MW00603795

The Encyclopedia Of Taekwon-Do Patterns

*The Complete Patterns Resource For Ch'ang Hon,
ITF & GTF Students Of Taekwon-Do*
Volume 3

CheckPoint
Press

The Encyclopedia Of Taekwon-Do Patterns

The Complete Patterns Resource For Ch'ang Hon, ITF & GTF Students Of Taekwon-Do

Volume 3

By Stuart Anslow

Warning

This book contains dangerous techniques which can result in serious injury or death. Neither the author nor publishers can accept any responsibility for any prosecution or proceedings brought or instituted against any person or body as a result of the use or misuse of information or techniques described or detailed within this book or any injury, loss or damage caused thereby. Some of the techniques and training methods described in this book require high levels of skill, control and fitness and should only be practiced by those in good health and under the supervision of a qualified instructor.

The Encyclopaedia Of Taekwon-Do Patterns

The Complete Patterns Resource For Ch'ang Hon, ITF & GTF Students Of Taekwon-Do

Volume 3

By Stuart Anslow
2nd Edition

Photographs by Kate Barry, Colin Avis & Stuart Anslow
Cover and Chapter Graphics by Jonathan Choi & Liam Cullen
Cover & Interior Layout by Stuart Anslow
Proof Read & Edited by Lyndsey Reynolds
Secondary Proof Reading by John Dowding

Copyright © 2010 Stuart Paul Anslow

All rights reserved

No parts of this publication may be reproduced, stored in a retrieval system, or transmitted in any form or by any means, electronic, mechanical, photocopying, recording or otherwise without the prior permission of the copyright owner.

British Library Cataloguing In Publication Data
A Record of this Publication is available
from the British Library

ISBN 978-1-906628-16-1

First Published 2010 by
CheckPoint Press, Dooagh, Achill Island, Co.Mayo, Republic of Ireland,
Tel: 00353 9843779   www.checkpointpress.com

In Memory Of
Grandmaster Trân Triêu Quân
1952 - 2010
Father, Husband, Teacher, President

Acknowledgements

I would like to express my gratitude to the following students and instructors of our wonderful art who have helped turn this collection of books into a reality.

First of all I would like to thank many of my own students who were involved in this project, some in multiple roles; Kate Barry and Colin Avis who both assisted me in taking the thousands of photographs, as well as being in them. Lyndsey Reynolds who proof read every page and posed for the Silla Knife Pattern chapter; Vikram Gautam, Parvez Sultan, Sushil Punj, Marek Handzel, Richard Baker and Jonathan Choi who all posed for various chapters as well, with Jonathan editing many of the various poses that accompany the start of each chapter, along with Liam Cullen (a friend rather than one of my own students) who also edited the graphics for the book covers, which is work that I could not do myself, as my initial attempts were poor to say the least.

I extend my gratitude and sincere thanks to my friends and fellow instructors Gordon Slater and Elliot Walker who posed for some of the chapters in these books, as well as John Dowding who performed a secondary proof read for me. Mr Slater also authored a great forward for this book series.

A big thank you to Master George Vitale, a true Taekwon-Do historian and researcher, for his most in-depth historical piece on the 'True' and 'Complete' history of Taekwon-Do, commissioned especially for these books (which can be found in appendix v, in Volume 1), as well as his help with research into the patterns, which along with Dani Steinhoff's research (thank you Dani) I was able to combine with my own to publish what I believe is the most definitive history of those Taekwon-Do pioneers that were involved in the actual creation of the individual patterns. I am very grateful to Gerald Robbins, creator of the Taekwondo Hall of fame website (www.taekwondohalloffame.com) for allowing me to use photographs from the site so that I could include as many recent photographs of these legendary pioneers as possible.

I would also like to express my appreciation to my friends; Yi, Yun Wook for assisting me in the correct hangul translations for each pattern, as well as the book title hangul and various bits of terminology. I am grateful to Master Paul McPhail (ITFNZ) for allowing me to use his work on the various motions employed by the ITF as well as a study on the sine wave and my friend Piotr Bernat for his help regarding the Global Taekwon-Do Federation (GTF) patterns featured in these books.

I extend my thanks to Master Keith Yates for clarifying the patterns of Grandmaster Jhoon-Rhee, Kevin McClear for clarifying the correct order of the patterns practiced by students of Grandmaster Hee, Il Cho as members of the Action International Martial Arts Association (AIMAA) and Daniel Gaul (Chun Kuhn Do) for clarifying the Kihap points used by Grandmaster Kim, Bok Man.

I also wish to thank a number of people who have contributed indirectly to this book, by either clarifying certain points for me, clarifying terminology or contributing in other ways. These people are Master Parm Rai (ITF), Master Ha Xuan (GTF), Master Earl Weiss (ITF), Stephen Gell (GTF), Art van der Lee (Oh Do Kwan), Patrick Steele (ITF), John A. Johnson (ITF), Philip Hawkins, Joseph Marrero, Chris Spiller (ITF) and Paul Mitchell (TAGB) - I thank you all as your input has shaped these books in some fashion.

Of course, I couldn't conclude these acknowledgements without thanking my instructors, David Bryan and John Pepper who set me on the right path and taught me most of the patterns I now practice and teach myself. And of course all those who helped pioneer the patterns founded by General Choi, Hong Hi, as well as Grandmaster Park, Jung Tae and Grandmaster Kim, Bok Man for the patterns they further devised, developed and instituted.

Foreword By Master George Vitale, 8th Degree

It is my pleasure to write this foreword for Mr. Stuart Anslow's latest gem, a book series on Taekwon-Do patterns. Mr. Anslow, a talented and dedicated martial artist and black belt instructor has made a name for himself in the martial art world as a steadfast defender of Taekwon-Do's ability to provide sound self defence skills to its students. The basis for his claim, which I steadfastly agree with, is to return to the roots of Taekwon-Do, when it was developed in the Republic of Korea's Army as an effective military means for self defence. This was during a period when strong defence skills were necessary to survive on the rough streets of Korea and during the protracted periods of war time that Korea was engaged in. The effectiveness of this new Korean martial art, a compilation of the fighting systems available at the time (1950s and 60s) has been well documented on the field of battle as well as reported in the periodicals of the day.

The soldiers who originally developed this Korean martial art were led by a legendary Major-General and Ambassador Choi Hong Hi, one of the founding members of the ROK Army. Gen. Choi over his lifetime (1918-2002) devised 25 patterns, called Tuls in Korean. These martial art 'forms', as many call them, are comprised as Gen. Choi would say, of "various fundamental movements, most of which represent either attack or defence techniques, set to a fixed and logical sequence". According to Gen. Choi training with these patterns will improve flexibility of your movements, build your muscles, assist with body shifting, help with one's breathing, develop fluid motions and allow for rhythmic movements that are aesthetically pleasing. Finally he felt that patterns provide a "critical barometer in evaluating an individual's technique".

Training with the patterns has become an important part of Taekwon-Do's syllabus for both promotion and competition. Additionally to not only helping to develop technical proficiency, diligent study and practice of these patterns is needed to help the student grow their mental or spiritual discipline. Adherence to the strict instruction of one's master instructor or the established criteria of competition allows the student numerous opportunities to enhance character traits necessary to build discipline. Knowledge of the meanings of the patterns and the great Korean patriots and significant events in Korean history that they are named after, also affords each student with fine examples to mentor and strive towards, which assists in developing their individual character further.

General Choi not only developed the original Taekwon-Do patterns, but he had the foresight to name them after these figures and events so details of Korea's history and culture would not only be spread around the world, but would be safeguarded against eradication, in case Korea ever suffered under the brutality of an occupying force again, as they were disseminated globally through his Taekwon-Do. These patterns became an important part in making his Taekwon-Do a distinctly Korean martial art. They, like other martial art forms, Katas, Poomsae or Hyungs, help to define their art. The Chang Hon patterns are like Gen. Choi's signature. Signatures are unique and much like another patriot, John Hancock, who signed America's Declaration of Independence in a large, bold way, allowing him to stand out during their late 18th century struggle for freedom. This is his fingerprint, his legacy, what he left behind as a gift for mankind for all of eternity. The 24 patterns he left us with reflect 24 hours, one day, or all of his life that he lived in the 20th century and into the next millennium.

These books cover not only the 24 patterns left to us by General Choi, but also Ko-Dang as well. This Tul, at times referred to as the lost pattern is contained within this work. The only other books to do this to my knowledge is the Patterns Handbook published by the United States Taekwon-Do Federation, which contains text instructions only and Hee Il Cho's Volume 3. The 39 moves of this pattern however are captured in this work with both photos and diagrams, in addition to the all important written instructions. Of course the older books written by General Choi contained just four of them in 1959 and only 20 in 1965. His other later books published through the International Taekwon-Do Federation (ITF) contained just 24, either with Ko-Dang or Juche, with none of them containing the detail that is presented here.

There have been other books on the Chang Hon patterns like the series of 5 books by Jhoon Rhee that only covered 9 color belt Hyungs up to red belt level. Hee Il Choi's series of 3 books still contain only the first 20 patterns developed by Gen. Choi and his soldiers. Never before have all 25 been covered in such detail. Additionally the 3 fundamental exercises required for promotion and advancement 4 direction punch, 4 direction block for 10th gup white belt beginners and 4 direction thrust for 2nd kup red belts are included as well.

These books also contain the Silla Knife pattern created by Grandmaster Kim Bok Man. Grandmaster Kim was a Sgt-Major under the command of Gen. Choi in the ROK Army. He was a member of the historic Taekwon-Do demonstration team that first took Taekwon-Do abroad when they toured Vietnam and Taiwan in 1959. Sgt-Major

Kim also went to Malaysia in 1963 where he helped General Choi finalize 16 of the Chang Hon Tuls. He was responsible for helping Taekwon-Do spread through out South East Asia. This pioneer was also a founding member of the ITF in 1966 and now teaches his art of Chun Kuhn Do.

Finally Mr. Anslow's series of books feature the patterns devised by the late Grandmaster Park Jung Tae, often referred to as the People's Master and used by the Global Taekwon-Do Federation (GTF). It is believed that no other book contains these patterns. So this work is a great resource for GTF students, who also do the ITF patterns as well. Grandmaster Park was a key right hand man to General Choi throughout the 1980s, as the former ITF Secretary General and Chairman of the ITF Instruction Committee. He was instrumental in creating Juche, Taekwon-Do's final pattern and the most Korean of all of the original Tuls.

Stuart has included Kihap points as emphasized by various groups or instructors. His true history section helps to sort out the confused and muddied story of Taekwon-Do's development. He takes the time to credit the original pioneers for some of their many contributions, so his books are most inclusive, as should be and as few, if any are. The studies written by Master Paul McPhail, one of the ITF's most technically savvy researchers, will help students understand the ways of motion, that are often confusing and hard to understand.

As an instructor Stuart Anslow teaches and focuses on Chang Hon Taekwon-Do. He does not get bogged down by organizational constraints or the politics that often can be in play. Therefore his work transcends these boundaries. In the words of a Pioneer Grandmaster Rhee Ki Ha, instrumental in assisting with the development and the spread of Taekwon-Do worldwide and the first person promoted to IX Dan (9th Degree) by the principle founder, Gen. Choi, we are ITF, "International Taekwon-Do Family". These works, along with his previous work are major steps forward in uniting this original Taekwon-Do family. Unity within the Tae Kwon Do community is long overdue. When one studies this recent project and his past contributions, it becomes increasingly clear that we have so much more in common than that which separates us. We are after all one Art and in addition we share aspects with all Martial Arts. Unity among "ITF stylists" should come first, followed by all Tae Kwon Do groups. Then it will be easier to see how we are all "just martial artists". These books, like Mr. Anslow's previous works on the hidden applications of the patterns is a must have for any serious martial artist.

Foreword By Gordon Slater, 6th Degree

Patterns, Kata's, Forms, Drills, whatever you want to call them are a basis…a foundation of many of the martial arts in the present and the past.

So what are the benefits of performing and perfecting of patterns? Some will say; *"It is a method of putting individual techniques into a logical sequence, it is building muscle content to perform techniques, improving ones stances and applications. It is a attacking and defence system."*

I explain to my own students; *"Patterns are like learning a foreign language, each technique is an individual word within that language, but to speak the language you have to put the words into sentences, Patterns are forming those sentences to enable you to speak the language, perform the art."*

Like all traditional martial arts, Patterns have been handed down from founder to student, who eventually becomes a Master, Master to instructors, instructors to senior students and so on. Also like all martial arts in our modern world, splits occur within organisations. How big would the founding body that first came to these shores (the U.K.) be today if it were not for all the splits and the birth of new organisations?

Today many martial arts schools are becoming independent, or merely affiliated to other larger groups to allow some recognition. And then there is evolution, some groups have changed techniques within the patterns or modified them. Some have stayed with tradition. I am sure Masters could debate the pros and cons of change and tradition until the end of time.

"If it is not broken why fix it?" Vs *"If one doesn't change, one gets left behind."*

What I am trying to point out here, is the evident dilution of the patterns gene pool. Different groups many have a slight difference (or big difference depending how they view it) in the performance of different patterns. What this book had tried to encompass is most people's views. It is unbiased, it does not judge the rights and wrongs of each difference in start position, finish position, speed of technique, where to Kihap, sine wave, hip twist etc.

What it does do is try and show all Taekwon-Do styles a logical way of performing each technique. These books demonstrate, in printed form, extensive photographic sequences of all the Ch'ang Hon patterns. Use it as a guide, use it as a bible, use it how you wish. Right or wrong opinions collected together give you a better understanding of anything i.e. Politics, the best system of an attacking football team, how to get from A to B the quickest route etc. View this book with an open mind, please do not be blinkered.

Mr. Anslow has spent many an hour sourcing information and different opinions to enable him to produce these volumes. He has sought out Masters and students alike to get their views, and ask the questions of 'why and how?' in order to define the small differences and make them as accurate and applicable to all as possible. With all this knowledge, he has then burnt much midnight oil in putting it all together, something many of us want to do, but never quite get around to. Therefore I have nothing but praise for Mr. Anslow in his tireless work to produce these volumes. A job very well done. Congratulations!

Finally, with regards to rank. My views are; *"A belt does not say how good you are, only what grade you are."*.

"Don't dismiss an opinion because of rank, 40 years experience doesn't always mean they have the greater knowledge."

If you judge a person on indepth knowledge opposed to time served, then from my opinion Mr. Anslow is of Master status!

Thank you Mr. Anslow for allowing us to share your knowledge!

About The Author

Stuart Anslow received his black belt in the art of Taekwon-Do in 1994 and is now a 5th degree.

He is Chief Instructor of the renowned Rayners Lane Taekwon-do Academy, which was established in 1999 and is based in Middlesex, UK.

During his martial arts career, Stuart has won many accolades in the sporting arena, including national and world titles. His Academy is one of the most successful in the country winning numerous gold medals at every martial arts championship his students enter, a testament to his abilities as an instructor.

In 2000, Stuart won a gold and silver medal at Grandmaster Hee Il Cho's 1st AIMAA Open World Championships in Dublin, Ireland and in 2004 he returned with 14 of his students to the 2nd AIMAA Open World Championships where they brought home 26 medals between them, 7 of them becoming World Champions in their own right, 2 became double world gold medallists, all from a single school of Taekwon-do.

In 2002, Stuart founded the International Alliance of Martial Arts Schools (IAOMAS) which drew martial artists from around the world together, growing from a few schools to over 400 in under a year. This non-profit organization is an online student and instructor support group that gives travelling students the ability to train at over hundreds of affiliated schools worldwide and is truly unique in the way it operates.

Stuart has been a regular writer for the UK martial arts press, having written many articles for 'Taekwon-do and Korean Martial Arts', 'Combat', 'Martial Arts Illustrated' and 'Fighters' magazines, as well as taking part in interviews for some of them. His numerous articles (which can now be found on the Academy web site) cover the many related subjects of martial arts from training to motivation, but his main love is Taekwon-do.

As well as his Academy, Stuart is the Chief martial arts instructor for two local schools (one private, one comprehensive), one of which was the first school in the country to teach martial arts as part of its national curriculum.

In 2002, Stuart received an award from the Hikaru Ryu Dojo, a martial arts academy in Australia, presented by their Chief Instructor and fellow IAOMAS member Colin Wee when he visited Stuart's Academy in the UK. In recognizing Stuart's contribution, Colin stated (referring to IAOMAS) that "*nothing to date has been so foresighted and effective as Stuart's work in establishing this worldwide online martial arts community.*"

In October 2003, Stuart was inducted into the world renowned Combat Magazines '*Hall Of Fame 2003*' for his work within the field of martial arts on a worldwide level. Combat magazine is the UK and Europe's biggest martial arts publication.

In 2004 he was selected as the Assistant Coach for the Harrow Borough Karate team, to compete at the prestigious London Youth Games held at Crystal Palace and has held this position ever since. During the same year Stuart also received various Honorary awards for his work in the International field of martial arts. From the USA he received a '*Yap Suk Dai Ji Discipleship*' award for his innovative work within IAOMAS and '*T'ang Shou*' society award for promoting martial arts on a worldwide scale.

In 2006 he was presented with a '*Certificate Of Appreciation*' from the members of IAOMAS Canada which read '*In recognition of your un-dying contribution to the evolution of martial arts and your inspirational and innovative formation of the International Alliance Of Martial Art Schools*'. Though just a humble instructor or student as he refers to himself, he continues to inspire others.

Also in 2006 he released his first book relating to Taekwon-do; '*Ch'ang Hon Taekwon-do Hae Sul: Real Applications To The ITF Patterns*' which explored the applications of patterns techniques contained within the Ch'ang Hon patterns, away from what was considered the '*norm*' for applications in favour of more realistic (and ultimately more beneficial) techniques. The book was extremely well received and became an instant success, seen as a 'must have' by both instructors and students worldwide.

In 2009, his love for Taekwon-do and disappointment with the coverage in the various Taekwon-do magazines led him to publish his own online magazine '*Totally Tae Kwon Do*'; a free, downloadable magazine for all students of the art. Supported by his friends, Tae Kwon Do instructors and students around the world it too became a worldwide success.

Stuart is well known in the UK and internationally and apart from being a full time instructor of Taekwon-do, teaching at local schools and running Self Protection courses for groups associated with his local Council, he is the father of four beautiful children, one with Downs Syndrome, whom he supports and cherishes to the best of his ability, despite his hectic work schedule.

Though a full time instructor, his reputation is gained not only by his own career but also by his uncompromising approach to teaching and the standards within his Academy and that of his students. The students quality are testament of his '*no short cuts*' approach to how martial arts in general and Taekwon-Do in particular, should be taught. His classes flourish with quality students despite much local competition from schools with a more *relaxed* approach to teaching and gradings. Many of his senior students feature in the photographs within this book.

Chloe, Callum, Logan and Jorja Anslow

Table Of Contents

Introduction

Originally it was my wish to produce a single book covering all the patterns in the Ch'ang Hon system, but sadly it was not to be as the cost would have been too prohibitive, so it was divided into three volumes.

So this series of books has come together to be a comprehensive reference for all students of Taekwon-do that follow the Ch'ang Hon system originally devised by General Choi, Hong Hi, including those that parted ways during Taekwon-do's history to date. This means they are suitable as a reference guide not just for those in the ITF (International Taekwon-Do Federation), but for those in organisations that are no longer connected to the ITF, such as the USTF, GTF, UITF, GTI, TAGB, AIMAA, BUTF, PUMA or indeed any Organisation, Federation, Association, Club, School, Academy or group that follows the patterns listed in this book; *The Ch'ang Hon Patterns*, *Blue Cottage Forms*, *ITF Patterns* or *Chon-Ji Forms* as they are also known. These books also include the Global Taekwon-Do Federation's Hyung's (the preferred term of Grandmaster Park, Jung Tae) and Silla knife pattern; patterns which were created or devised by pioneering instructors along the same lineage stemming from General Choi and are thus now part of the Taekwon-Do worlds collection of patterns.

Taekwon-Do's history stretches from before 1955 (when it was actually named) to the present and a consequence of this is that there are various styles of the art which were the pinnacle of the Ch'ang Hon system at certain points in time. For example, a student who's instructor started teaching in the 1970's and continues to teach the way he was taught will learn and perform slightly different from a student who's instructor started in the 1990's or one that is very current with any ITF changes. When writing these books I wanted to take this into account, so rather than simply show things the way I teach or learned them I enlisted help from some instructors that have come from different lines to me and thus perform their patterns slightly differently and as such, the various time periods are represented as well. As the books are designed to be an encyclopedia for all students of Taekwon-Do rather than students from a particular organisation I felt it was a good idea to have the various stages/differences represented. Throughout the book, the students and instructors that pose for the various photographs have performed, trained and/or taught patterns within the UKTA, ITF, GTI, TAGB and BUTF and as well as independently, thus representing a large portion of students throughout the world who perform them in a similar manner.

The Taekwon-do world has many organisations, each having minor differences with how they do things. For example, one organisations L-Stance may be slightly different in width than another's or some will execute a Forefist Punch using 'hip twist', while others will use 'sine wave' etc. and so the differences in *basics* can be numerous. However, all organisations that can trace their roots back to General Choi have one constant and that is the patterns themselves; as although an L-Stance may be of a slightly different width, or the way they move between techniques may be different, in the main, with a few minor exceptions (which I have tried to note in these volumes), the actual techniques each organisations students execute within each of the 25 Ch'ang Hon patterns remain pretty much the same. It is with this in mind that I wrote these books. It differs from other books of this type as it doesn't tell you how you *must* perform the basics (though it gives examples) or how long or wide your stances *must* be or whether to use sine-wave or hip twist, it simply tells you what each move is, what stance it is in and just as importantly, how to get from one technique to another.

Over the years there have been many good books published on the Taekwon-do patterns, many of which I own. Indeed General Choi himself has written both the 15 volume encyclopedia, as well as a condensed version. However, the former is expensive and hard to get and the latter only details the patterns in text form, with few pictures, neither of which contain the pattern *'Ko-Dang'* which many Taekwon-do students are required to learn and practice. Consequently, those books that do contain *'Ko-Dang'* do not contain the pattern *'Juche'* which again, many students need to learn and practice. In some organisations *'Juche'* replaced *'Ko-Dang'*, while others never instituted *'Juche'* to begin with. To complicate matters more, years later, some organisations once again replaced *'Juche'* back with the original *'Ko-Dang'*, with one organisation renaming *'Juche'* to *'Ch'ang Hon'* (ICTF) and another renaming it to *'Ko-Dang'* (ITF under Grandmaster Choi, Jung Hwa) despite keeping all the moves the same. These books include both *'Ko-Dang'* and *'Juche'* to cover this gap.

Furthermore, some of the earlier released books while good, only contained the first 20 patterns but over the years, General Choi developed a total of 25 Ch'ang Hon patterns and this book includes them all. These books also include the 3 Saju exercises he developed which rarely appear in other books. Only *Saju Jirugi'* and occasionally *'Saju Makgi'* have been documented in other books, but these books also include *'Saju Tulgi'*.

Some pioneering instructors who once helped developed the original patterns went on to institute or develop their own. In order to make this book collection a true *Encyclopedia Of Taekwon-Do Patterns* I have included these as well. Apart from the historical merit these patterns have, it is important for those students in the GTF (Global Taekwon-Do Federation) as they have to learn 30 patterns in total and as yet, I haven't seen any books that show them at all, so I hope I have done them justice. These are the six *'Jee-Goo Hyung'* developed by Grandmaster Park, Jung Tae. Though some simply call them the *new GTF patterns* others refer to them as *Jee-Goo hyung* because *Jee-Goo* means *Global*.

I have also included the *'Silla Knife Pattern'*, instituted by legendary Taekwon-Do instructor Grandmaster Kim, Bok Man because it is one of the most requested patterns I have come across on various Taekwon-Do internet forums, possibly because some schools wish to add a weapons form but want one that is Korean based with the added benefit that it comes from such a pioneering instructor. Grandmaster Kim, Bok Man instituted many additional forms for his own students, both empty handed and weapon based forms but the *Silla Knife Pattern* is the only one which is mentioned. That said, I would have liked to include more, but space did not permit it so I have represented this great master with the Silla Knife Pattern.

Aside from having a complete collection of patterns in a single set of books, a small bug-bear of mine is that previous patterns books often show individual pictures of each move within each pattern (of the ones they cover), from the point of view of an examiner watching you. This is fine (and is the way I have also laid out these books) until the student is travelling back to his or her start position and facing away from the examiner, where by many books simply show a photo of the pattern performers back and you cannot even see the technique at all - this has been corrected in these volumes as most techniques have a full size, forward facing shot.

One of the biggest problems I have seen with virtually all *'step by step'* pattern books is that while decent, they are not really a true *'step by step'* guide. They simply show each technique at its final stage, then the next and the next etc. but they never actually show you how to get from one to another, how to execute the actual technique fully, the chamber positions and how your feet move with the various spins, pivots and slides. This for many students is very confusing. In these books I have tried to correct this by showing the movements from one technique to another by way of multiple pictures of the performer moving between techniques and nearly every technique is covered in this way.

Coupled with the *'step by step'* photographs, each movement is described in text form, along with directional arrows and detailed foot diagrams, showing both previous and current foot positions to make it even easier for the first time performer of a pattern to grasp them. On occasion, when one *count* is actually two movements (for example move #12 of Hwa-Rang tul is both a Side Piercing Kick and a Knifehand Strike), these have further been split into 'A' and 'B' shots in order to show the performance of the whole movement.

These volumes also list many of the minor differences in various organisations, such as the various motions used by the ITF, Kihap points for those that utilise them, the actual order of patterns organisations require and a sine wave study.

As part of this book I wanted to have a section on the history of the patterns and pay homage to those that helped in their creation. Most know that General Choi, Hong Hi always had the final say on the patterns contained within his system, but many others helped devise them (to various degrees) and they have never been given full credit, so part of this book finally acknowledges their contribution to the patterns of Taekwon-do. I also wanted to include a 'History of Taekwon-Do' section, but as these books relate to just the patterns I included a 'Brief History' at the beginning of each volume, but also a more complete history section as an appendix in volume 1, which is possibly the most concise and researched, not to mention true history ever to appear in a Taekwon-Do book that isn't a history book per se.

Finally, I have not listed specific applications within these volumes because; firstly I know that when a student passes a grading and needs to learn a new pattern, the actual applications are very much secondary to learning the *pure* techniques of the pattern themselves. This is what I refer to as *'stage 1'* of patterns training, with *'stage 2'* being learning them in-depth, with as much detail as possible, which this book also covers. *'Stage 3 and 4'* are learning, applying and training realistic applications which are covered in the book *'Ch'ang Hon Taekwon-do Hae Sul: Real Applications To The ITF Patterns'*. Secondly, the sheer amount of information within these books on the patterns alone means there was little space for discussing applications anyway. As these are covered in my other book it seemed ultimately pointless trying to squeeze applications into these volumes. In any event, the ITF (as well as other organisations) already have various applications to the movements contained within their own patterns. Those who have already read *'Ch'ang Hon Taekwon-do Hae Sul'* will know my personal views regarding this particular issue, so I wouldn't feel comfortable listing standard applications as portrayed in certain other books. Finally of course, this series of books are for learning and performing solo patterns.

This second volume features all the Dan grade patterns in the Ch'ang Hon system of Taekwon-Do from *Po-Eun* (1st Dan) to *Yoo-Sin* (3rd Dan), used by both the *International Taekwon-Do Federation* (ITF) and other *Ch'ang Hon* based organisations, as well as the *Global Taekwon-Do Federation* (GTF) patterns required at the same Dan grade levels. It also features all both *Ko-Dang* and *Juche* so no matter which one your organisation requires it can be referenced here. I hope you find them a useful reference tool.

A Brief History Of Ch'ang Hon Taekwon-Do

Contrary to popular belief, Taekwon-Do is not a 2,000 year old Korean martial art and its connection to the ancient Korean art of Taek-Kyon is tenuous at best. It is in fact derived, for the most part, from Shotokan Karate. It also has other martial arts (such as Judo, Hapkido, Boxing, Wrestling and even Chinese Martial Arts influences) fused into what is now know as 'The Art of Hand and Foot' aka Taekwon-Do.

In 1945 Korea was liberated from the Japanese and Korea officially formed its armed forces (its modern military). Although Japanese martial arts remained being taught in Korea (by Korean instructors) in the various Kwan's (gyms), General Choi, Hong Hi wanted to break away from the arts of Japan, to have a martial art to train his soldiers in that had Korean values and at the same time instil national pride following the devastating effects of his country being occupied by Japan. He had learned Karate in Japan during the occupation of his country and had been teaching it to the soldiers under his command since 1946.

General Choi, Hong Hi

In 1954 during the Korean war, President Syngman Rhee saw a demonstration by the military Korean martial arts masters under General Choi's leadership and was so impressed he ordered that it be taught to all military personnel. This blessing from the president propelled Korean martial arts forward like a rocket. General Choi is known to have been teaching martial arts to his 29th Infantry Division on Cheju Island already and in 1954 he founded the Oh Do Kwan (Gym of My Way), along with Lieutenant Nam, Tae Hi, which was seen as the catalyst for the formation of Tae Kwon Do, as while General Choi taught the soldiers Karate he was, at the same time, formulating Taekwon-Do

President Syngman Rhee

Colonel Nam, Tae Hi

A unification effort was made to unite the various Kwans that were teaching in Korea, in order to make them a unified single Korean martial art and despite opposition, the art was officially named on the 11th of April 1955, known as the birth date of Taekwon-Do, a name put forward by General Choi. Despite this, for many years only General Choi's soldiers in the Oh Do Kwan and their civilian counter parts in the Chung Do Kwan used the term 'Tae Kwon Do'.

Photograph from the meeting when they named Taekwon-do with many martial arts masters present. General Choi can be seen at the head of the table. circa 1955

Naming this emerging art was simply the beginning, in fact even when officially named not one of the patterns were fully formulated, though in 1955 the first Ch'ang Hon pattern (Hwa-Rang) was finished. Over time Tae Kwon Do moved further away from its Karate roots by devising more new patterns, named after Korean historical figures or events; emphasising the rising and dropping into techniques (which was later termed sine-wave) as opposed to the Karate way of keeping the head the same height throughout; and of course introducing many more kicking techniques. Eventually, Taekwon-Do broke the chains of its roots and became distinct in its own right.

Even though Taekwon-Do has evolved into a martial art for all, including a large sport based side, it should be remembered that it was formulated as an art of self-defence, by soldiers, for soldiers and its effectiveness was no more evident than when it was actually used on the battle fields of Vietnam, where it was so feared by the Viet Cong that soldiers were told to avoid engaging in combat, even when Korean soldiers were unarmed, due to their knowledge of Taekwon-do![1]

Taekwon-Do is one of only a few martial arts that have a proven, battlefield tested, track record. Following the battle of Tra Binh Dong,[2] Times magazine ran an article that stated *"It was knife to knife and hand-to-hand—and in that sort of fighting the Koreans, with their deadly tae kwon do (a form of karate), are unbeatable. When the action stopped shortly after dawn, 104 enemy bodies lay within the wire, many of them eviscerated or brained"*[3].

> (On the night of St. Valentine's Day, a North Vietnamese regiment of 1,500 men struck at the 254 man Korean Company.)
> *It was knife to knife and hand-to-hand and in that sort of fighting the Koreans, with their deadly (a form of Tae kwon Do), are unbeatable. When the action stopped shortly after dawn, 104 enemy bodies lay within the wire, many of them eviscerated or brained. All told, 253 Reds were killed in the clash, while the Koreans lost only 15 dead and 30 wounded.*
> —Time— 24 Feb 1967

'A Savage Week'. Time Magazine, 24 February 1967

1959 was an influential year for Taekwon-Do as well as the start of the Vietnam war. The Korean Taekwon-Do Association (KTA) was formed, an armed forces demonstration team toured Taiwan and South Vietnam and General Choi published his first book on the art of Taekwon-Do and in 1962 the first Taekwon-Do tournament was held.

1962 was also the year that General Choi was forced to retire from the military due to his lack of support for President Park, Jung Hee who took power following a bloodless coup in 1961. Instead, General Choi was made an Ambassador and shipped off to Malaysia where he continued to teach and formulate Taekwon-Do, which included formulating 15 more Ch'ang Hon patterns.

General Choi finally returned to Korea in 1964 only to find that, due to politics, the Korean Taekwon-Do Association (KTA) had ceased to exist and had been replaced with the Korean Tae Soo Do Association (KTA) which was formed in 1962. However, in 1965 General Choi was elected as President of the KTA and managed to return the name to the Korean Taekwon-Do Association. He also published his second book on Taekwon-Do and lead a demonstration team around South East Asia and Europe. This demonstration tour was called the 'Kuk Ki Taekwon-Do Good-will Mission'!

On the 22nd March, 1966 General Choi formed the International Taekwon-Do Federation in Seoul, South Korea, with Master Kim, Jong Chan designing both the ITF badge (logo) and the ITF flag.

---

[1] 'Captured Viet Cong orders now stipulate that contact with the Koreans is to be avoided at all costs unless a Viet Cong victory is 100% certain. Never defy Korean soldiers without discrimination, even when are not armed, for they all well trained with Taekwondo.' - An excerpt from an enemy directive seized. - July 22, 1966

[2] A full transcript of the battle of Tra Binh Dong, including how Taekwon-Do was used in it to great effect, can be found in the book *'Ch'ang Hon Taekwon-do Hae Sul'* by the same author.

[3] 'A Savage Week', Time Magazine, 24 February 1967

As General Choi became more and more opposed (and vocal) to President Park's regime he eventually self-exiled himself to Canada in 1972, where he also relocated the ITF headquarters, as well as publishing his third book on Taekwon-Do (known as the Bible of Taekwon-Do). This was the first book to contain all of the 24 patterns of Taekwon-Do.

Taekwon-Do's history is full of politics and it was due to this that the International Taekwon-Do Federation (ITF) headquarters relocated to Canada instead of staying in Korea. It was due to politics that General Choi exiled himself to Canada in 1972 and it was politics that lead to the formation of the World Taekwondo Federation (WTF) in 1973. Sadly, politics has plagued Taekwon-Do all through it short life and continues to do so to this day, even after General Choi passed on the 15th June, 2002.

To read a more in-depth history of Taekwon-Do, please read *'The True And More Complete History Of Taekwon-Do'*, written especially for this book by Taekwon-Do researcher and historian Master George Vitale - it can be found as appendix v, in Volume 1.

Further to this, if you enjoy learning about the history of Taekwon-Do then I wholeheartedly recommend the following books:

A Killing Art: The Untold History Of Tae Kwon Do
by Alex Gillis

The Korean Martial Art Of Tae Kwon Do & Early History
by Grandmaster Choi, Chang Keun

The Taegeuk Cipher
by Simon John O'Neill

Finally, though I have learned a lot by studying these patterns to ensure they are as correct as possible, I have come to realize just what a momentous task General Choi executed by putting together the original *'Encyclopedia of Taekwon-Do'* as, even with the digital age this was a difficult task, so I can only imagine what it was like in 1983 and just how difficult a task it was with just a 35mm camera and a type writer, even with some of the most gifted and hard-working students (aka the pioneers), the Taekwon-Do world will ever see.

The True History Of The Ch'ang Hon Patterns

The patterns of Ch'ang Hon Taekwon-Do are the signature of the systems creator General Choi Hong Hi. When Taekwon-Do was officially named on 11th April, 1955 not one of the final 24 patterns of Ch'ang Hon Taekwon-do had been finalized, as at this time Taekwon-do still used the Kata from its father art of Shotokan Karate, though this was due to change.

Of course all pattern development was overseen by General Choi himself. He had major technical input into them as well as the final word on them, he was like the director, but other Masters acted out the movements and added their input which helped immensely in their formulation, but they have never received proper credit for it, until now.

(2 Star) General Choi, Hong Hi

Colonel Nam, Tae Hi

A popular misconception is that the patterns were created in order, from *Chon-Ji* onwards, but actually the first official pattern ever devised was *Hwa-Rang*, which was created with the help of Colonel Nam, Tae Hi and Sergeant Han, Cha Kyo in 1955. *Choong-Moo* was the second pattern created in 1955, again with the help of Colonel Nam, Tae Hi, with the third pattern created for the Ch'ang Hon Taekwon-do system being *Ul-Ji* which again, was created with the help of Sergeant Han, Cha Kyo in 1957. Sometime prior to 1958/59 pattern *Sam-Il* was created by General Choi (with the help of the soldiers of the Oh Do Kwan) and it was included in his first book on Taekwon-Do, published in 1959.

It wasn't until 1961 that the next pattern would be finalised. This would be pattern *Ge-Baek* and it was created with the help of Master C.K.Choi, another soldier.

Sergeant Han, Cha Kyo

When General Choi was sent to Malaysia in 1962 fifteen more patterns were created, bringing the total to twenty. It was between 1962 and 1964, with the assistance of his soldiers Master Woo, Jae Lim and Master Kim, Bok Man (who attained the highest non-commissioned officer rank of Sgt. Major) that patterns *Chon-Ji, Dan-Gun, Do-San, Won-Hyo, Yul-Gok, Joong-Gun, Toi-Gye, Kwang-Gae, Po-Eun, Ko-Dang, Choong-Jang, Choi-Yong, Yoo-Sin, Se-Jong* and *Tong-Il* were created, although the actual order is unclear.

Master C.K. Choi

Sometime around 1968 patterns *Eui-Am, Moon-Moo, Yon-Gae* and *So-San* were formulated with the assistance of Master Cho, Sang Min, bringing the final number of patterns to '24', General Choi's ideal number. Master J.C. Kim, Master Park, Jong Soo and Master Lee, Byung Moo among others, may also have helped formulate these patterns.

Master Woo, Jae Lim

Following a trip to North Korea in the early 1980's to secure support for the ITF, pattern *Ko-Dang* was removed and replaced with a new pattern called *Juche*. The reasons for this are discussed all over the internet, as are the merits or demerits of it all. However, whatever ones point of view is, the simple fact remains that it was changed by the founder himself and thus around 1981 pattern *Juche* was created and became an official ITF pattern between 1983 to 1985. It is believed that Master Park, Jung Tae played a major role (if not the major role) in the development of pattern *Juche*, along with assistance form Master Choi, Jung Hwa (General Choi's son), Michael McCormack (General Choi's son-in-law) and Master Lim, Won Sup.

Just prior to this trip, Master Kim, Bok Man, who helped with the formulation of at least 15 patterns in Malaysia between 1962 and 1964 released a book which shows he introduced 4 new patterns for his students called the Silla patterns. These consisted of two empty hand patterns, one knife pattern and a pole pattern. Many believe that Master Kim, Bok Man was opposed to Taekwon-do being a totally empty handed system and wished to have weapons included in its curriculum. The Silla patterns are said to come from the time of the Hwa-rang warriors who existed during the Silla Dynasty in Korea, hence their name.

Master Kim, Bok Man

In 1990 Master Park, Jung Tae parted company with General Choi and the ITF. Up until this point he had been the ITF Secretary-General as well as Chairman of the ITF Instruction Committee, and the man responsible for teaching virtually all Taekwon-do techniques and how they were executed and performed. In 1990 Master Park, Jung Tae formed the Global Taekwon-do Federation (GTF) and further developed six new patterns, often referred to as the *Jee-Goo hyung*. Students within this federation now perform 30 patterns in total including all the original Ch'ang Hon patterns (with *Ko-dang* rather than *Juche*), along with the six new patterns created by Master Park.

Master Cho, Sang Min

As a consequence of Master Park, Jung Tae leaving the ITF the sine-wave motion changed once again. The previous up/down motion was changed to a newer down/up/

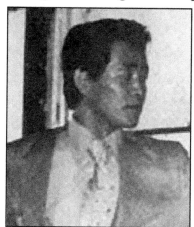

down motion and later refined to a relax/up/down motion by some organisations, however it is still referred to as *'sine wave'* forcing practioners of the original or older version to rename what they do as *'Natural Motion'*.

In 2005 the International Ch'ang Hon Taekwon-Do Federation (ICTF) renamed pattern *'Juche'* as *'Ch'ang Hon'* after General Choi's penname and in 2009, the ITF under Grandmaster Choi, Jung Hwa renamed pattern *'Juche'* as *'Ko-Dang'*, however the movements in both cases remain the same as the original pattern *Juche*.

Master J.C. Kim

It should be noted that I have referred to those who helped in the formulation of the Ch'ang Hon patterns by the term Master, when some are now actually Grandmasters. This is not a sign of disrespect for them, but rather a sign of respect for those whose status I do not know.

Though often referred to as the ITF patterns, their correct name is the *Ch'ang Hon* patterns. *Ch'ang Hon* was the pseudonym of General Choi and means *'Blue Cottage'*, so sometimes they are referred to as the *Blue Cottage* patterns or even the *Chon-Ji* patterns, after the first pattern in the set.

Master Park, Jong Soo

Originally they were referred to by their Korean name of *Hyung*, which means *form,* but General Choi later changed this terminology to *tul*, which means *pattern*, as he felt it was a better description of them and was a uniquely Korean term. Master Park, Jung Tae preferred to use the term *hyung*, so when describing his patterns I follow suit, as I have also done with Master Kim, Bok Man's *Silla pattern*, as that was the terminology he chose to use.

Master Lee, Byung Moo

Finally, it is interesting to note that originally, all the patterns were named after famous Korean historical figures or groups, except the first and last ones. The first pattern, *'Chon-Ji'* represents the creation of the world, therefore the creation of Korea as well as the beginning for Taekwon-do students. The last pattern, *'Tong-Ill'* represents the reunification of North and South Korea which was General Choi's lifelong dream; the beginning and the end so to speak. With the change of *'Ko-Dang'* to *'Juche'* however, this changes the equation slightly, but I feel the names of the first and last patterns in the set were highly significant to General Choi and his Korean heritage and ideals.

Master Park, Jung Tae

In an interview conducted in 1999 General Choi was asked how long it took to research his patterns, to which he replied *"I began my research in March 1946 into what was to be named Taekwon-do on April 11, 1955. My research ended in 1983. The patterns represent my study of the Art in this period."*

Sadly Master Han, Cha Kyo passed in 1996, Master Park, Jung Tae passed away on the 11th April, 2002; 47 years to the day that Taekwon-Do was officially named and General Choi passed away on 15th June 2002. Each has left an enduring mark in Taekwon-do's history and between them they have left their legacy of Taekwon-Do with us.

Differences Between Organisations

Different Taekwon-Do organisations often require their students to perform basic movements in a way that is particular to that organisation. This is mostly due to the time period that the Taekwon-Do organisation base their patterns on i.e. When they separated paths from the ITF or another group, and though there can be minor differences in the way certain techniques are executed, such as aligning a forefist punch with the shoulder, rather than the centre of the body, in the main, these differences are minute and will easily be honed by your own instructor to organisational requirements.

With that said, there are two main areas that do vary from association to association; these are the way blocks are chambered and the way a student moves from one stance to the next and its these differences we detail here. It should be noted that none of them are unequivocally the right way and consequently, none are incorrect either, it is all down to organisational preference.

Chambering Positions When Executing Blocking Techniques

Across the organisations of Taekwon-Do there are 3 main ways that blocks (and some strikes) are chambered. For the examples below we will use the chambering position of a *Left Low Outer Forearm Block*:

A. Wrist to Wrist - A student would align the back of his left wrist, above (or on top) of his left wrist, to the side of his body and execute the block from this position.

B. Forearm to Forearm - A student would align the his left outer forearm above the lower portion of his right outer forearm (sometimes referred to as inside the forearm), to the side of his body and execute the block from this position.

C. Far Back - A student would bring his blocking arm (in this case the left arm) as far back as is possible, bringing it around the body as far as he can reach. For low block this would mean above the shoulder, to the side and execute the block from this position.

Chambering Positions When Executing Striking Techniques

Punch and Backfist Chambering Positions

Most organisation execute closed fist striking techniques from similar positions, with minor variations.

Punches are usually executed from the hip, whereas back fists and knifehand strikes are executed from similar positions as blocks; from the side of the body.

Palm and Knifehand Chambering Positions

Palm techniques are usually executed from the chest, however some organisations execute them from the hips.

Fingertip thrusts are also mostly executed from chest height, however some organisations execute them from the hips.

Straight Fingertip Thrust, Flat Fingertip Thrust and Upset Fingertip Thrust Chambering Positions

*Older Straight Fingertip
Thrust Chamber Position*

In some Taekwon-Do organisations they still use the older chambering motion for a Straight Fingertip Thrust, where the thrusting hand starts from the hip, comes up slightly and shoots forwards (similar to pulling and pointing a pistol from a cowboy style holster).

Knifehands

One quite big difference that needs to be noted relates to knifehands and how they are chambered and travel to their point of impact. Many organisations form the knifehand position from the offset; opened and formed at the chamber position and allow it to travel relaxed but formed to its point of impact. However, some organisations, specifically ITF ones, require the student to chamber a knifehand as a closed fist which travels towards it target relaxed but still closed, only opening into the knifehand at the last possible moment. This applies to both knifehand blocks and knifehand strikes.

Above And Below Show The Two Different Methods Of Executing A Knifehand Strike

Ways Of Moving Between Stances

As with chambering blocks there are various ways of moving from one stance to the next that the various Taekwon-Do organisations require. These are usually related to a specific time period in Taekwon-Do's development and are down to organisational preference. There are 3 main ways of moving:

A. Horizontal Wave - This method sees the student travelling from one stance to the next keeping their head at the same height, with little or no vertical movement. The knees are bent to compensate for the rising of the body as the student moves from one stance to the next. This method is usually utilized by organisations that separated from the ITF in its early years.

B. Natural Motion - This methods sees the students travelling in a natural way from one stance to the next. It allows the natural raising of the body as the student moves forwards before dropping into the technique. This method usually incorporates hip twist as well (see above) and was originally called 'sine-wave' but was changed by some pioneers as a way to distinguish it from the newer version of sine-wave detailed next. This method is usually utilized by organisations that separated from the ITF in the mid 80's or early 90's.

C. Sine-Wave - This method sees the student dropping slightly (or relaxing as some term it) just prior to the start of the movement, then rising as they move forwards before finally dropping into the technique. This method is usually utilized by organisations that remain part of the ITF following the departure of Master Park Jung Tae in the early 90's.

Stepping Between Stances

Like the vertical motions (or lack of) employed when stepping forwards or backwards between stances, the motion the feet travel in also varies and can be separated into 3 distinct methods. In these examples we use the transfer from a left walking stance, stepping forwards into a right walking stance.

A. **In & Out** - This method sees the students right foot travel in so it is next to the left foot, before moving outwards again into the stance.

B. Skating - This method, commonly referred to as *skating* sees the students right foot travel in a small arc as it moves forwards. At a maximum it comes only half a shoulder width in, but usually it is much less than that.

C. Parallel - This method see the student move forwards without moving his foot in at all, as if walking along a set of train tracks.

Spot-Turning / Centre-Line Turns

There are many ways of turning that General Choi employed in the patterns which are referenced in the relevant chapters, however the most common one found is *'Spot-Turning'* (Gujari Dolgi) or as many know it; a *'Centre-Line Turn'* as seen between moves #2 and #3 in Do-San tul and many other places.

Different organisations perform them differently, with some stepping straight across the centre-line and simply turning around (left diagram on page 19), with others moving the front foot 'in' and 'back' before turning and then moving the (now) front foot forwards again (right diagram on page 19). For the sake of uniformity, in these books they are named *'Centre-Line Turns'*.

Methods of Spot Turning/Centre Line Turns

Hip Twist, Sine Wave And Knee-Springs

The two ways that many organisations utilize when striking or blocking are hip twist or sine-wave, with a third way being a combination of the two. These are separate from the *Ways Of Moving Between Stances* as they refer to ways blocks or strikes are executed with or without the forward momentum of moving the whole body. These methods are used when both moving or stationary, with the addition of 'Knee-Spring' that some organisations used for executing techniques stationary, as explained below:

A. Hip Twist - This involves holding the hip back as a student moves or executes a technique before finally flicking it forwards at the last moment to add power into the strike or block. This method is often utilized in conjunction with the horizontal wave (detailed previously). When stationary (as in the pictures above) a student simply withdraws the hip back, then shoots it forwards again as they strike or block.

B. Sine-Wave - A student would drop into a stance to execute a technique and rely solely on the sine-wave relax/up/down motion to add power into the technique without additional hip twist. When stationary (as in the pictures on the previous page) the student simply relaxes, rises and drops again while executing the strike or block. This method is almost specifically used by current ITF students.

C. Combination - The final method is a combination of both the previous methods and utilizes dropping into stance's as well as hip twist to add power. The student would rise naturally as they move or use a knee-spring if stationary (see below), holding the hip back slightly, before flicking it into place as the student drops and executes the technique. This method is most often used in conjunction with the *Natural Motion* way of moving.

Knee-Spring

A knee-spring is utilized by some organisations when executing stationary techniques. It sees the student raising their rear heel and relaxing their rear knee; a slight rising of the body is often seen, as is some hip twist but both are minimal compared to using sine-wave or hip twist alone. As the technique is executed, the rear heel thrusts back to the floor and the rear knee locks straight creating forward power for the block or strike.

How To Use This Book

The main pages of this book are laid out in a specific way in order to transmit as much information as possible to the student. Students have various combinations in the way they like to learn; some can relate straight away to pictures, others like pictures combined with text etc.

Each of the main chapters start with an introduction page, displaying the name of the pattern itself, its standard definition, its diagram and the number of movements it contains.

Nopunde Bakat Palmok Yop Makgi
High Outer Forearm Side Block

The pages of each patterns chapter (as well as the saju's) displays two or three large numbered pictures of the movement in each patterns sequence. This is combined with various arrows (which are detailed overleaf), which show direction of movement, transition of stances and head (facing) direction amongst other things.

The majority of all the main pictures are shown forward or side facing so techniques can be seen clearly, but where a movement is facing away, a smaller picture appears inset in the main picture to show the correct facing direction it should be executed in. All patterns are shot as if being watched by an examiner.

Underneath the main picture is the terminology of the movement in both Korean and English, and underneath this is a foot diagram showing the previous foot positions as *greyed out* and the new foot positions as black footprints. Below this the movements are described in text form, for example:

32. Pivot your left foot 90 degrees anti-clockwise into a *Left Walking Stance*, whilst executing a *High Outer Forearm Side Block* with your left arm.

Finally, at the bottom of each page are a number of small pictures showing how to move from the previous technique to the next, for all the techniques listed on that page. These include the movements in the correct facing direction, as well as chambers and various parts of the transitions from one move to the next.

Previous

Moves 31, 32 & 33

The arrows that accompany the main pictures represent the following:

A *large solid arrow* shows the *direction of movement* from one stance to the next in the form of a step (either forwards, backwards or other direction) or a kick.

A *large dashed arrow* shows the *facing direction* following a movement where there is more than just a simple step involved. A *dashed arrow* is used to show that the footwork is more detailed and thus needs to be looked at within the written descriptions. An example of this would be the 2nd movement of Saju Jirugi that has you turning 90 degrees to block, but the foot of the rear leg travels backwards, in the opposite direction to where you are facing. Other examples would be changing from one stance to another without a step forwards, spot-turning/centre-line turns, a step backwards, a spin or a foot shift such as the 2nd and 3rd movements of Won-Hyo tul, where you only shift your front foot forwards from an L-Stance to form a fixed stance.

If there are *no arrows*, then there is no change of stance and no forwards or backwards movement and it is simply an execution of another technique. For example, the Low Block and Rising Block combination in Dan-Gun tul.

Two arrows together show direction of movement while facing another direction, for example, the Back Fist Strike in Toi-Gye tul. The *larger arrow* represents the direction of movement (which may or may not be dashed as detailed above), while the *shorter dashed arrow* represents the way you face upon completion or during execution of the technique.

Finally, a *short dashed arrow* on its own indicates the facing direction of a movement if it changes from the previous movement but doesn't have a step involved. For example, the Low Reverse Knifehand Blocks in Ge-Baek tul, where the stance remains the same, but the facing changes to the opposite side.

Stances and foot positions are represented by footprints upon a rectangle:

The *rectangle* represents the average length and width of a basic Walking Stance, with other stances as slight variations on them. They are incorporated to show how the feet are repositioned in relation to the previous stance of a technique/move. They are used in conjunction with foot prints to show foot placement, with a dashed rectangle with *light foot prints* representing the previous foot positions of the last stance used and *dark foot prints* representing the current foot positions of the new stance or position. The example to the left shows how the student steps from a Right Walking Stance into a Right L-Stance.

On some pages a *boxed piece of text* holds information for students who follow specific systems and holds information pertinent to

| ITF Note: ..... |

them, that may be of use as a general note as well. They give information relating to certain sets of movements, for example if combinations are performed in various motions such as Connecting, Continuous, Fast Motion etc.

Finally, at the back of each book are tables relating to pattern orders used by many of the big associations (as they do vary), Kihap points that some organisations use, as well as an in-depth description of various motions and a sine wave study for those that utilise it.

Standards For The Performance Of Patterns

No matter which organisation you practice under, there are a number of standards or rules that are applicable to the way patterns are executed as a solo exercise and include the Saju exercises. These are as follows:

1. **All patterns start and finish on the same spot.**

2. **Each pattern should be performed in a rhythmic motion without stiffness.**

3. **Each technique should be fully formed before moving onto the next.**

4. **Techniques should be performed with realism.**

5. **Correct breathing should be performed throughout each pattern.**

6. **Correct posture and muscle tension should be utilized in all techniques.**

7. **Each pattern should be perfected before moving onto the next.**

Finally, all students of Taekwon-do should remember that *patterns are a series of defensive and offensive movements, set in a logical order against one or more imaginary opponents* and as such, are a core element of Taekwon-Do and its related self defence.

Though there are many benefits to practicing patterns, such as health, flexibility and balance etc., learning them to simply pass a grading or win a medal at a competition is the least important factor of patterns, as without understanding and appreciating them fully, they become little more than a dance routine - and there is so much more to them!

Choi-Yong
14th Century Commander In Chief

최 영 틀

Choi-Yong has 46 movements. Choi-Yong is named after General Choi Yong, Premier and Commander in Chief of the armed forces during the 14th century Koryo Dynasty. Choi Yong was greatly respected for his loyalty, patriotism and humility. He was executed by his subordinate commanders headed by General Yi Sung Gae, who later became the first King of the Lee Dynasty.

Moa Junbi Sogi 'C'
Closed Ready Stance 'C'

**Kaunde Palmok
Daebi Makgi**
Middle Forearm Guarding Block

**Joongi Joomok
Nopunde Jirugi**
*High Middle Knuckle
Fist Punch*

1. From *Closed Ready Stance 'C'*, move your Left foot forwards to form a *Right Rear Foot Stance* and execute a *Middle Forearm Guarding Block*.

Note: The direct translation of *'Moa'* is actually *'Close'*, but most use the terminology *'Closed'*, so I have stayed with the most common term used throughout this book.

2. Maintain your stance and execute a *High Middle Knuckle Fist Punch* with your Left fist.

From the ready posture to moves 1 & 2

**Kaunde Palmok
Daebi Makgi**
*Middle Forearm
Guarding Block*

**Joongi Joomok
Nopunde Jirugi**
*High Middle Knuckle
Fist Punch*

Sonkal Chookyo Makgi
Knifehand Rising Block

3. Perform a centre-line turn into a *Left Rear Foot Stance* and execute a *Middle Forearm Guarding Block*.

4. Maintain your stance and execute a *High Middle Knuckle Fist Punch* with your Right fist.

5. Perform a centre-line turn into a *Left Walking Stance* while executing a *Knifehand Rising Block* with your Left hand.

Previous

Moves 3, 4 & 5

Dollimyo Makgi
Circular Block

Kaunde Ap Joomok Jirugi
Middle Forefist Punch

Sonkal Chookyo Makgi
Knifehand Rising Block

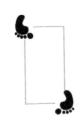

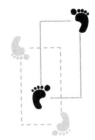

6. Maintain your stance and execute an *Inner Forearm Circular Block* with your Right arm.

7. Maintain your stance and execute a *Middle Forefist Punch* with your Left fist.

8. Perform a centre-line turn into a *Right Walking Stance* while executing a *Knifehand Rising Block* with your Right hand.

Previous   *Moves 6, 7 & 8*

Dollimyo Makgi
Circular Block

Kaunde Ap Joomok Jirugi
Middle Forefist Punch

**Najunde Sonkal
Daebi Makgi**
*Low Knifehand
Guarding Block*

9. Maintain your stance and execute an *Inner Forearm Circular Block* with your Left arm.

10. Maintain your stance and execute a *Middle Forefist Punch* with your Right fist.

11. Perform a centre-line turn into a *Right L-Stance* while executing a *Low Knifehand Guarding Block* .

Previous

Moves 9, 10 & 11

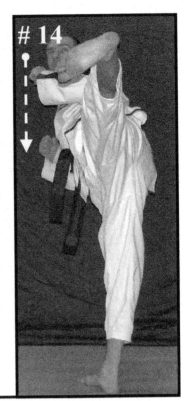

Kaunde Dollyo Chagi
Middle Turning Kick

Nopunde Bandae Dollyo Goro Chagi
High Reverse Hooking Kick

Kaunde Yop Cha Jirugi
Middle Side Piercing Kick

Note: Movements 13 & 14 are performed as *'Consecutive Kicks'*

12. Execute an angled *Middle Turning Kick* (30 degrees) with your Right leg, before lowering to the side and slightly in front of your Left foot.

13. Execute a *High Reverse Hooking Kick*, straight in front of you with your Left leg.

14. Without placing the kicking leg down, immediately execute a *Middle Side Piercing Kick* with your Left leg.

Previous   *Moves 12, 13 & 14*

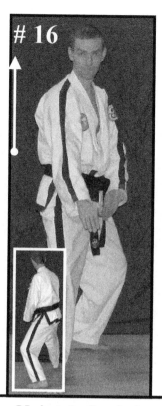
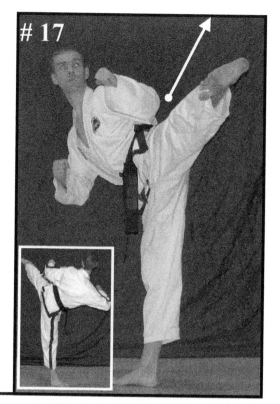

Ap Palkup Taeragi
Front Elbow Strike

Najunde Sonkal Daebi Makgi
Low Knifehand Guarding Block

Kaunde Dollyo Chagi
Middle Turning Kick

15. Following the kick, lower your Left foot to form a *Left Walking Stance* while executing a *Front Elbow Strike* with your Right elbow, striking your Left palm as you do so.

16. Perform a centre-line turn into a *Left L-Stance* while executing a *Low Knifehand Guarding Block*.

17. Execute an angled *Middle Turning Kick* (30 degree) with your Left leg, before lowering it to the side, slightly in front of your Right foot.

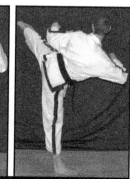

Previous   *Moves 15, 16 & 17*

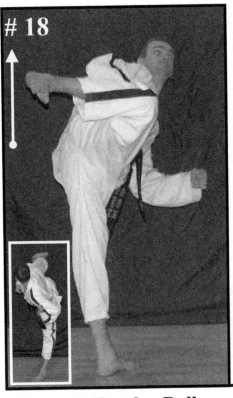

Nopunde Bandae Dollyo Goro Chagi
High Reverse Hooking Kick

Kaunde Yop Cha Jirugi
Middle Side Piercing Kick

Ap Palkup Taeragi
Front Elbow Strike

Note: Movements 18 & 19 are performed as *'Consecutive Kicks'*

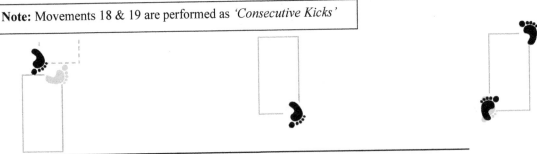

18. Execute a *High Reverse Hooking Kick*, straight in front of you with your Right leg.

19. Without placing the kicking leg down, immediately execute a *Middle Side Piercing Kick* with your Right leg.

20. Following the kick, lower your Right foot to form a *Right Walking Stance* while executing a *Front Elbow Strike* with your Left elbow, striking your Right palm as you do so.

Previous   *Moves 18, 19 & 20*

Sonbadak Noollo Makgi
Palm Pressing Block

Sonbadak Noollo Makgi
Palm Pressing Block

Sonkal San Makgi
Knifehand W Block

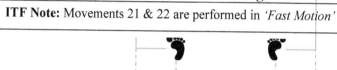

ITF Note: Movements 21 & 22 are performed in *'Fast Motion'*

21. Move forwards into a *Left Walking Stance* while executing a *Right Palm Pressing Block*.

22. Move forwards into a *Right Walking Stance* while executing a *Left Palm Pressing Block*.

23. Move your Right foot backwards, just past your Left foot, then pivot 180 degrees anti-clockwise on your Right foot to form a *Left Walking Stance* and execute a *Knifehand W Block*.

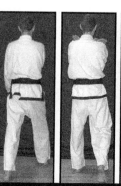

Previous   *Moves 21, 22 & 23*

Kaunde Yop Cha Jirugi
Middle Front Snap Kick

**Kaunde Palmok
Daebi Makgi**
Middle Forearm Guarding Block

24. Keeping your hands in the position of the last block, execute a *Middle Front Snap Kick* with your Right leg.

25. Lower the kicking leg to the rear to form a *Right L-Stance* while executing a *Middle Forearm Guarding Block*.

Previous

Moves 24 & 25

Sonkal San Makgi
Knifehand W Block

Kaunde Yop Cha Jirugi
Middle Front Snap Kick

26. Move your Right foot forwards to form a *Right Walking Stance* while executing a *Knifehand W Block*.

27. Keeping your hands in the position of the last block, execute a *Middle Front Snap Kick* with your Left leg.

Previous

Moves 26 & 27

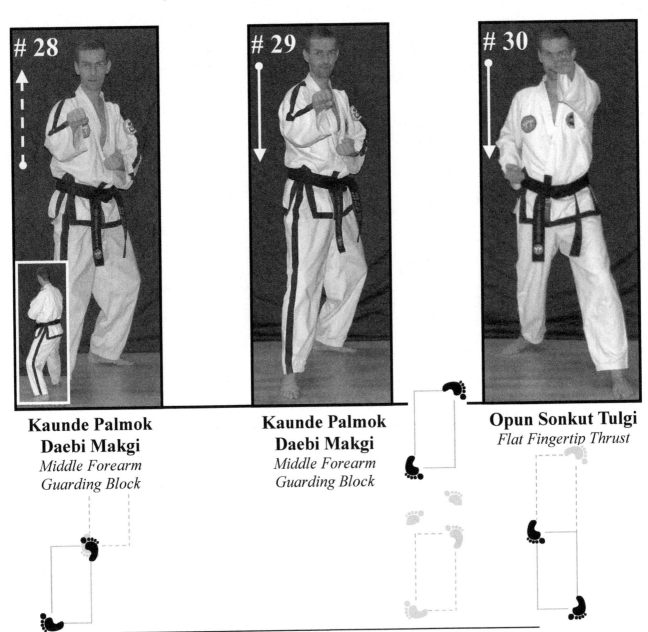

Kaunde Palmok
Daebi Makgi
Middle Forearm
Guarding Block

Kaunde Palmok
Daebi Makgi
Middle Forearm
Guarding Block

Opun Sonkut Tulgi
Flat Fingertip Thrust

28. Lower the kicking leg to the front, then pivot 180 degrees clockwise on your Right foot to form a *Left L-Stance* while executing a *Middle Forearm Guarding Block*.

29. *Take a double step forwards* before pivoting clockwise and sliding backwards to form *a Left L-Stance* while executing a *Middle Forearm Guarding Block*.

30. Move forwards into a *Left Walking Stance* and execute a *Flat Fingertip Thrust* with your Left hand.

Previous   *Moves 28, 29 & 30*

Opun Sonkut Tulgi
Flat Fingertip Thrust

Sonbadak Golcha Makgi
Palm Hooking Block

**Kaunde Ap
Joomok Jirugi**
Middle Forefist Punch

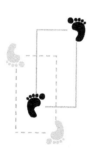

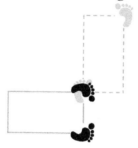

31. Perform a centre-line turn into a *Right Walking Stance* and execute a *Flat Fingertip Thr*ust with your Right hand.

32. Pivot 90 degrees clockwise on your Left foot, moving your Right foot to form a *Parallel Stance* while executing a *Middle Palm Hooking Block* with your Right hand.

33. Maintain your stance and execute a *Middle Forefist Punch* with your Left fist.

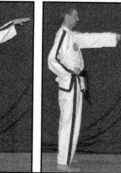

Previous

Moves 31, 32 & 33

Goburyo Junbi Sogi 'A'
Bending Ready Stance 'A'

Kaunde Yop Cha Jirugi
Middle Side Piercing Kick

34. Pivot 180 degrees on your Left foot, forming a *Left Bending Ready Stance 'A'* in the opposite direction.

35. From the previous stance, execute a *Middle Side Piercing Kick* with your Right leg, pulling your arms into a *Forearm Guarding Block* as you execute the kick.

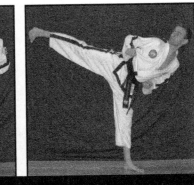

Previous   *Moves 34 & 35*

**Dung Joomok
Nopunde Yop Taeragi**
Back Fist High Side Strike

Nopunde Bandae Dollyo Goro Chagi
High Reverse Hooking Kick

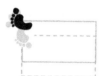

36. Following the kick, lower your Right leg and jump forwards to form a *Right X-Stance* while executing *Back Fist High Side Strike* with your Right fist, bringing the finger belly of your Left hand to the side of your fist.

37. Execute a *High Reverse Hooking Kick* with your Right leg in the opposite direction (180 degrees).

Moves 36 & 37

Sonkal Yop Taeragi
Knifehand Side Strike

Sonbadak Golcha Makgi
Palm Hooking Block

Kaunde Ap Joomok Jirugi
Middle Forefist Punch

 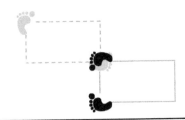 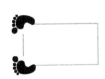

38. Following the kick, lower Right foot in a *stamping* motion to form a *Left L-Stance* while executing a *Right Knifehand Side Strike*.

39. Pivot 180 anti-clockwise on your Right foot and move your Left foot to form a *Parallel Stance* while executing a *Middle Palm Hooking Block* with your Left hand.

40. Maintain your stance and execute a *Middle Forefist Punch* with your Right fist.

Previous   *Moves 38, 39 & 40*

Goburyo Junbi Sogi 'A'
Bending Ready Stance 'A'

Kaunde Yop Cha Jirugi
Middle Side Piercing Kick

41. Pivot 180 degrees anti-clockwise on your Right foot, forming a *Right Bending Ready Stance 'A'* facing the opposite direction.

42. From the previous stance, execute a *Middle Side Piercing Kick* with your Left leg, pulling your arms into a *Forearm Guarding Block* as you execute the kick.

Previous   *Moves 41 & 42*

Dung Joomok Nopunde Yop Taeragi
Back Fist High Side Strike

Nopunde Bandae Dollyo Goro Chagi
High Reverse Hooking Kick

43. Following the kick, lower your Left leg and jump forwards to form a *Left X-Stance* while executing *Back Fist High Side Strike* with your Left fist, bringing the finger belly of your Right hand to the side of your fist.

44. Execute a *High Reverse Hooking Kick* with your Left leg in the opposite direction (180 degrees).

Previous

Moves 43 & 44

Sonkal Yop Taeragi
Knifehand Side Strike

Kaunde Ap Joomok Jirugi
Middle Forefist Punch

45. Following the kick, lower your Left foot in a *stamping* motion to form a *Right L-Stance* while executing a *Left Knifehand Side Strike*.

46. *Slide* forwards into a *Right Fixed Stance* executing a *Middle Forefist Punch* with your Right fist.

Previous   *Moves 45 & 46*

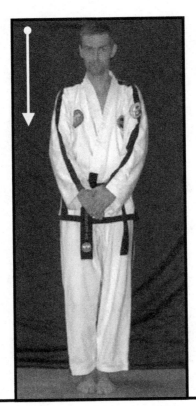

Moa Junbi Sogi 'C'
Closed Ready Stance 'C'

Return. Bring your Right foot back to the ready posture *(Closed Ready Stance 'C')*.

Move 46 & return to ready position

Tips For Choi-Yong Tul

1. Following the Turning Kicks at 30 degrees (moves #12 and #17) ensure you lower your foot past your centre line to enable you to perform the Reverse Hooking Kicks (moves #13 and #18) properly.

2. Keep your knee high when transitioning from the Reverse Hooking Kicks (moves #13 and #18) to the Side Piercing kicks (moves #14 and #19).

3. The Palm Pressing Blocks (moves #21 and #22) are performed in a motion that simply looks like you are walking forward and performing the blocks as you do so i.e. There is no stopping between the two techniques or stances involved.

4. Remember, following the first Front Snap Kick (move #24) the foot is placed behind while facing forwards, but following the second Front Snap Kick (move #27) the foot is lowered in front as part of the turn (so it still ends up to the rear).

5. It is hard to see when in book form, but the Double Step motion on move #29 is performed in a very relaxed matter. Those that are watching this pattern for the first time (at a competition for example) often think the performer has forgotten the pattern, given up and is walking away as it is so relaxed. They then realise its actually part of the pattern as they turn and slide into the L-Stance with Forearm Guarding Block.

Pyong-Hwa
Peace

평

화

형

Pyong-Hwa means *'Peace'*. Grandmaster Park, Jung Tae dedicated this pattern to the United Nations Organisation (UNO). This pattern has 50 movements to symbolize the 50 countries which found the United Nations Organisation in San Francisco, USA in 1950, after the 2nd World War. The diagram represents peace.

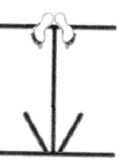

Charyot Junbi Sogi 'B'
Attention Ready Stance 'B'

**Kaunde Sonkal
Daebi Makgi**
Middle Knifehand Guarding Block

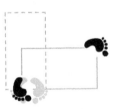

1. From *Attention Ready Stance 'B'*, move your Left foot to the side to form a *Right L-Stance*, while executing a *Middle Knifehand Guarding Block*.

From the ready posture to move 1

Kaunde Ap Cha Busigi
Middle Front Snap Kick
(Slow Motion)

Nopunde Ap Cha Busigi
High Front Snap Kick
(Slow Motion)

Note: Movements 2a & 2b are performed as *'Consecutive Kicks'*

2a. Taking your weight on your Right foot, execute a *Middle Front Snap Kick* with your Left leg. Perform in slow motion.

2b. Without placing your Left foot down, execute a *High Front Snap Kick* with your Left leg. Perform in slow motion.

Previous   *Moves 2a & 2b*

Sonkal Chookyo Makgi
Knifehand Rising Block

Bandalson Nopunde Bandae Taeragi
Arc-Hand High Reverse Strike

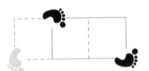

2c. Following the previous kick, lower your Left foot down in front, then move forwards with your Right foot to form a *Right Walking Stance* while executing a *Knifehand Rising Block* with your Right hand.

3. Maintain your stance and execute an *Arc-Hand High Reverse Strike* with your Left hand.

Previous

Moves 2c & 3

**Kaunde Sonkal Dung
Daebi Makgi**
*Middle Reverse Knifehand
Guarding Block*

Kaunde Yop Cha Jirugi
Middle Side Piercing Kick
(Slow Motion)

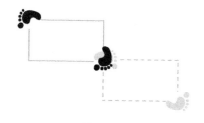

4. Pivot 180 degrees clockwise, moving your Right foot to form a *Left L-Stance* while executing a *Middle Reverse Knifehand Guarding Block*.

5a. Taking your weight on your Left foot, execute a *Middle Side Piercing Kick* with your Right leg. Perform in slow motion.

Previous　　　　　　　*Moves 4 & 5a*

 # 5b

Nopunde Yop Cha Jirugi
High Side Piercing Kick
(Slow Motion)

5b. Without placing your Right foot down, execute a *High Side Piercing Kick* with your Right leg. Perform in slow motion.

Previous   *Move 5b*

Bakat Palmok Chookyo Makgi
Outer Forearm Rising Block

**Pyon Joomok Nopunde
Bandae Jirugi**
Open Fist High Reverse Punch

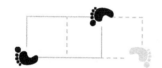

5c. Following the previous kick, lower your Right foot down in front, then move forwards with your Left foot to form a *Left Walking Stance* while executing a *Outer Forearm Rising Block* with your Left arm.

6. Maintain your stance and execute an *Open Fist High Reverse Punch* with your Right hand.

Previous   *Moves 5c & 6*

Nopunde Bandae Dollyo Chagi
High Reverse Turning Kick

Kaunde Ap Joomok Jirugi
Middle Forefist Punch

Najunde Sonkal Makgi
Low Knifehand Block

7a. Taking your weight on your Right foot, execute a *High Reverse Turning Kick*, 90 degrees anti-clockwise from your current position, with your Left leg.

7b. Following the previous kick, lower your Left leg to form a *Right L-Stance* while executing a *Middle Forefist Punch* with your Right fist.

8. Take a double step forwards by first moving your Right foot next to your Left, then moving your Left foot forwards to form a *Left Walking Stance* while executing a *Low Knifehand Block* with your Left hand.

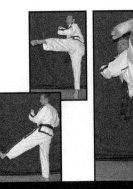

Previous   *Moves 7a, 7b & 8*

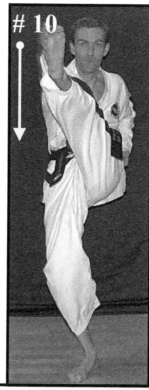

Sondung Bakuro Taeragi

Back-Hand Outward Strike

Nopunde Bandal Chagi

High Crescent Kick

Nopunde Yop Cha Tulgi

High Side Thrusting Kick

Note: Movements 10 & 11 are performed as *'Consecutive Kicks'*

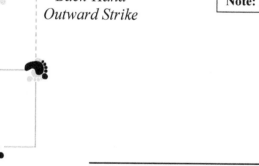

9. Move your Right foot forwards in a *stamping* motion to form a *Left L-Stance* while executing a *High Back-Hand Outward Strike* with your Right hand.

10. Execute a *High Crescent Kick* with your Left leg to your Right palm.

11. Without placing your Left foot down, re-chamber and execute a *High Side Thrusting Kick* with your Left leg.

Previous

Moves 9, 10 & 11

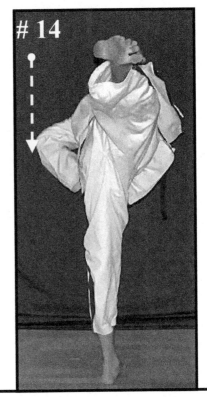

Sondung Bakuro Taeragi
Back-Hand Outward Strike

Nopunde Bandal Chagi
High Crescent Kick

Nopunde Yop Cha Tulgi
High Side Thrusting Kick

Note: Movements 13 & 14 are performed as *'Consecutive Kicks'*

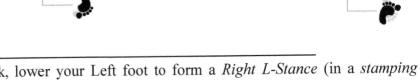

12. Following the previous kick, lower your Left foot to form a *Right L-Stance* (in a *stamping* motion) while executing a *High Back-Hand Outward Strike* with your Left hand.

13. Execute a *High Crescent Kick* with your Right leg to your Left palm.

14. Without placing your Right foot down, re-chamber and execute a *High Side Thrusting Kick* with your Right leg.

Previous   *Moves 12, 13 & 14*

Gutja Makgi
9-Shape Block

Twimyo Yop Cha Jirugi
Flying Side Piercing Kick

Kaunde Sonkal Daebi Makgi
Middle Knifehand Guarding Block

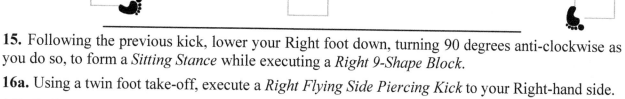

15. Following the previous kick, lower your Right foot down, turning 90 degrees anti-clockwise as you do so, to form a *Sitting Stance* while executing a *Right 9-Shape Block*.

16a. Using a twin foot take-off, execute a *Right Flying Side Piercing Kick* to your Right-hand side.

16b. Following the previous kick, land in a *Left L-Stance* while executing a *Middle Knifehand Guarding Block*.

Previous   *Moves 15, 16a & 16b*

**Twimyo Ap
Cha Busigi**

Flying Front Snap Kick

**Kaunde Palmok
Daebi Makgi**

*Middle Forearm
Guarding Block*

Nopunde Dwitcha Jirugi
High Back Piercing Kick

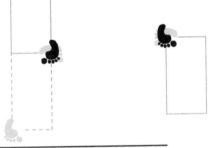

17. Using a twin foot take-off, jump backwards (but remain facing forwards) and execute a *Flying Front Snap Kick* with your Left leg.

18. Following the previous kick, land in a *Right L-Stance* while executing a *Middle Forearm Guarding Block*.

19a. Taking your weight on to your Right leg, execute a *High Back Piercing Kick* to your rear (180 degrees) with your Left leg.

Previous   *Moves 17, 18 & 19a*

Sonkal Yop Taeragi
Knifehand Side Strike

Moa Junbi Sogi 'B'
Closed Ready Stance 'B'

Sang Palmok Makgi
Twin Forearm Block

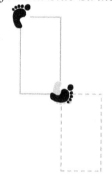

19b. Following the previous kick, lower your Left leg to form a *Right L-Stance* (in the direction your were kicking) while executing a *Middle Knifehand Side Strike* with your Left hand.

20. Bring your Right foot to your Left foot to form a *Closed Ready Stance 'B'*.

21. Pivoting 90 degrees anti-clockwise, move your Left foot out to form a *Right L-Stance* while executing a *Twin Forearm Block*.

Previous   *Moves 19b, 20 & 21*

Nopunde Bandal Jirugi
High Crescent Punch

Nopunde Yop Cha Jirugi
High Side Piercing Kick

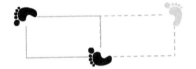

22. Move your Right foot forwards to form a *Right Walking Stance* while executing a *High Crescent Punch* with your Left fist.

23. Execute a *High Side Piercing Kick* with your Left (rear) leg.

Previous   *Moves 22 & 23*

Ap Palkup Taeragi
Front Elbow Strike

Sang Sonkal Makgi
Twin Knifehand Block

24. Following the previous kick, lower your Left leg in front to form a *Left Walking Stance* while executing a *Right Front Elbow Strike* to your Left palm.

25. Move foot to foot by bringing your Left foot to your Right foot; turning 180 degrees clockwise as you move your Right foot forwards to form a *Left L-Stance* while executing a *Twin Knifehand Block*.

Previous — *Moves 24 & 25*

Bandae Opun Sonkut Tulgi
Reverse Flat Fingertip Thrust

Nopunde Dollyo Chagi
High Turning Kick

26. Move your Left foot forwards to form a *Left Walking Stance* while executing a *High Reverse Flat Fingertip Thrust* with your Right hand.

27. Execute a *High Turning Kick* with your Right leg.

Previous   *Moves 26 & 27*

Wi Palkup Taeragi
Upper Elbow Strike

**Sonkal Najunde
Daebi Makgi**
Low Knifehand Guarding Block

Kaunde Bituro Chagi
Middle Twisting Kick

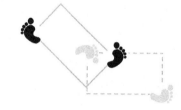

28. Following the previous kick, lower your Right leg in front to form a *Right Walking Stance* while executing an *Upper Elbow Strike* with your Left elbow.

29. Move foot to foot by bringing your Right foot to your Left foot; turning 135 degrees anti-clockwise as you move your Left foot forwards to form a *Right L-Stance* while executing a *Low Knifehand Guarding Block* at a 45 degree angle.

30. Execute a *Middle Twisting Kick* with your Right leg.

Previous

Moves 28, 29 & 30

Nopunde Dollyo Goro Chagi
High Hooking Kick

Nopunde Yop Cha Jirugi
High Side Piercing Kick

Note: Movements 31a & 31b are performed as *'Consecutive Kicks'*

31a. Following the previous kick, lower your Right foot in front and execute a *High Hooking Kick* with your Left leg.

31b. Without placing your Left foot down, re-chamber and execute a *High Side Piercing Kick* with your Left leg.

Previous

Moves 31a & 31b

Nopunde Bakuro Gutgi
High Outward Cross-Cut

Sonkal Najunde Daebi Makgi
Low Knifehand Guarding Block

Kaunde Bituro Chagi
Middle Twisting Kick

32. Following the previous kick, *stamp* your Left leg in front to form *a Right L-Stance* while executing a *High Outward Cross-Cut* with your Left hand.

33. Move foot to foot by bringing your Left foot to your Right foot; turning 90 degrees clockwise as you move your Right foot forwards to form a *Left L-Stance,* while executing a *Low Knifehand Guarding Block* at a 45 degree angle.

34. Execute a *Middle Twisting Kick* with your Left leg.

Previous   *Moves 32, 33 & 34*

Nopunde Dollyo Goro Chagi
High Hooking Kick

Nopunde Yop Cha Jirugi
High Side Piercing Kick

Note: Movements 35a & 35b are performed as *'Consecutive Kicks'*

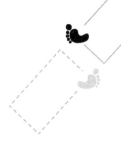

35a. Following the previous kick, lower your Left foot in front and execute a *High Hooking Kick* with your Right leg.

35b. Without placing your Right foot down, re-chamber and execute a *High Side Piercing Kick* with your Right leg.

Previous   *Moves 35a & 35b*

Nopunde Bakuro Gutgi
High Outward Cross-Cut

Sang Sonbadak Noollo Makgi
Twin Palm Pressing Block

Digutja Jirugi
U-Shape Punch

36. Following the previous kick, lower your Right leg in front (in a *stamping* motion) to form *a Left L-Stance* while executing a *High Outward Cross-Cut* with your Right hand.

37. Move foot to foot by bringing your Right foot to your Left foot; straightening up to face your start position. Then move your Left foot out and forwards to form a *Left Diagonal Stance*, while executing a *Twin Palm Pressing Block*.

38. Move foot to foot by bringing your Left foot to your Right foot, then move your Right foot forwards to form a *Right Fixed Stance* while executing a *U-Shape Punch*.

Previous — *Moves 36, 37 & 38*

Suroh Chagi
Sweeping Kick

Kaunde Dwitcha Jirugi
Middle Back Piercing Kick

Kaunde An Palmok Makgi
Middle Inner Forearm Block

39a. Execute a *Sweeping Kick* with your Left foot.

39b. Following the previous kick (sweep) lower your Left foot in front and execute a *Middle Back Piercing Kick* with your Right leg.

40. Following the previous kick, lower your Right foot in front to form a *Left L-Stance* while executing a *Middle Inner Forearm Block* with your Right arm.

Previous   *Moves 39a, 39b & 40*

Goburyo Junbi Sogi 'A'
Bending Ready Stance 'A'
(Slow Motion)

Kaunde Yop Cha Jirugi
Middle Side Piercing Kick
(Slow Motion)

41. Taking your weight on your Right foot, pivot 270 degrees anti-clockwise raising your Left leg to form a *Bending Ready Stance 'A'*.

42. Without placing your Left foot down, execute a *Middle Side Piercing Kick* with your Left leg. Perform in slow motion.

Previous   *Moves 41 & 42*

Nopunde Yop Cha Jirugi
High Side Piercing Kick
(Slow Motion)

43. Without placing your Left foot down, re-chamber and execute a *High Side Piercing Kick* with your Left leg. Perform in slow motion.

Previous

Move 43

Nopunde Dollyo Goro Chagi
High Hooking Kick

Note: Movements 42, 43 & 44 are performed as *'Consecutive Kicks'*

44. Without placing your Left foot down, execute a *High Hooking Kick* with your Left leg. Perform in normal/fast motion.

Previous   Move 44

Kaunde Sewo Jirugi
Middle Vertical Punch

Goburyo Junbi Sogi 'A'
Bending Ready Stance 'A'
(Slow Motion)

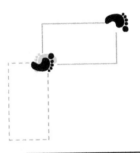

45. Following the previous kick, lower your Left foot in front to form a *Left Walking Stance* while executing a *Middle Vertical Punch* with your Right fist.

46. Move foot to foot by bringing your Left foot to your Right foot; turning 180 degrees clockwise and raise your Right leg to form a *Left Bending Ready Stance 'A'*.

Previous

Moves 45 & 46

Kaunde Yop Cha Jirugi
Middle Side Piercing Kick
(Slow Motion)

47. Without placing your Right foot down, execute a *Middle Side Piercing Kick* with your Right leg. Perform in slow motion.

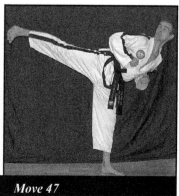

Previous

Move 47

Nopunde Yop Cha Jirugi
High Side Piercing Kick
(Slow Motion)

48. Without placing your Right foot down, re-chamber and execute a *High Side Piercing Kick* with your Right leg. Perform in slow motion.

Previous   Move 48

Nopunde Dollyo Goro Chagi
High Hooking Kick

Note: Movements 47, 48 & 49 are performed as *'Consecutive Kicks'*

49. Without placing your Right foot down, execute a *High Hooking Kick* with your Right leg. Perform in normal/fast motion.

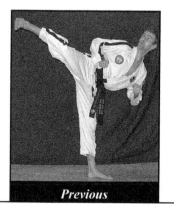

Previous   *Move 49*

**Nopunde Ghin Joomok
Bandae Jirugi**
High Long Fist Reverse Punch

Charyot Junbi Sogi 'B'
Attention Ready Stance 'B'

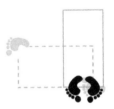

50. Following the previous kick, lower your Right foot in front to form a *Right Walking Stance* while executing a *High Long Fist Reverse Punch* with your Left fist.

Return. Bring your Right foot backwards to *Attention Ready Stance 'B'*.

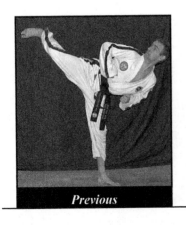

Previous

Move 50 & back to Ready Posture

Tips For Pyong-Hwa Hyung

1. This pattern has a lot of slow motion high, section kicking techniques in it, so extra leg strength training may prove useful so the techniques can be executed both slowly and with accuracy.

Yon-Gae

General Yon Gae Samoon

Yon-Gae is named after a famous General during the Koguryo Dynasty, Yon Gae Somoon. Yong-Gae has 49 movements which refer to the last two figures of 649 A.D, the year he forced the Tang Dynasty to quit Korea after destroying nearly 300,000 of their troops at Ansi Sung.

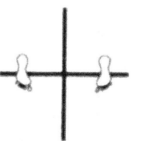

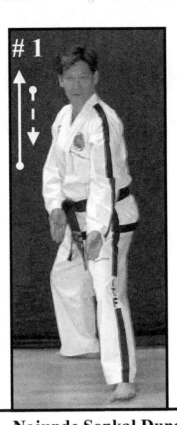

Moosa Junbi Sogi 'A'
Warrior Ready Stance 'A'

**Najunde Sonkal Dung
Daebi Makgi**
*Low Reverse Knifehand
Guarding Block*

**Nopunde Ghin
Joomok Jirugi**
*High Long Fist Punch
(slow motion)*

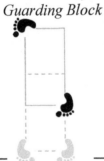

1. From *Warrior Ready Stance 'A'*, slide backwards approximately half a stance (from your front foot) with your Right leg, to form a *Right L-Stance* while executing a *Low Reverse Knifehand Guarding Block* in a circular motion.

2. Shift your back (Right) foot to form a *Left Walking Stance* and execute a *High Long Fist Punch* with your Right fist. Perform in slow motion.

Hand Position

From the ready posture to moves 1 & 2

Kaunde Palmok
Daebi Makgi
Middle Forearm
Guarding Block

Twimyo Sonkal Yop Taeragi
Flying Knifehand Side Strike

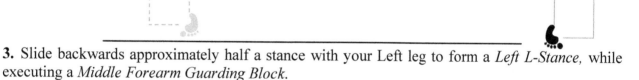

3. Slide backwards approximately half a stance with your Left leg to form a *Left L-Stance,* while executing a *Middle Forearm Guarding Block.*

4a & 4b. Jump up and forwards approximately one stance length, executing a *(Flying) Knifehand Side Strike* whilst in the air landing in a *Left L-Stance,* while keeping the Knifehand Side Strike extended.

Previous　　　　　　　　　　　*Moves 3 & 4*

**Kyocha Joomok
Momchau Makgi**
X-Fist Checking Block

Nopunde Bakuro Gutgi
High Outward Cross-Cut

**Sun Palkup
Naerjo Tulgi**
*Straight Elbow
Downward Thrust*

5. Shift backwards (approx. 6 inches) while maintaining the previous *Left L-Stance* and execute a *X-Fist Checking Block*.

6. Slip your Right foot to form a *Right Walking Stance* while executing a *High Outward Cross-Cut* with your Right hand.

7. Pull your Right foot back to form a *Left Rear Foot Stance* and execute a *Straight Elbow Downward Thrust* with your Right elbow.

Previous   *Moves 5, 6 & 7*

**Nopunde Dung
Joomok Taeragi**
High Back Fist Strike

**Najunde Bandae Bakuro
Sonkal Makgi**
*Low Reverse Outward
Knifehand Block*

**Sonbadak Golcha
Makgi**
Palm Hooking Block

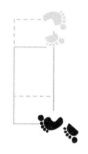

8. Jump forwards a stance length into a *Left X-Stance*, executing a *High Back Fist Strike* with your Left fist.

9. Move your Right foot backwards to form a *Left Walking Stance* while executing a *Low Reverse Outward Knifehand Block* with your Right hand.

10. Bring your Right foot in line with your left foot to form a *Parallel Stance* and execute a *Middle Palm Hooking Block* with your Left hand.

Previous   *Moves 8, 9 & 10*

Kaunde Ap Joomok Jirugi
Middle Forefist Punch

Najunde Sonkal Dung Daebi Makgi
Low Reverse Knifehand Guarding Block

Nopunde Ghin Joomok Jirugi
High Long Fist Punch (slow motion)

11. Maintain your stance and execute a *Middle Forefist Punch* with your Right fist.

12. Slide backwards approximately half a stance (from your front foot) with your Left leg, to form a *Left L-Stance* while executing a *Low Reverse Knifehand Guarding Block* in a circular motion.

13. Shift your back (Left) foot to form a *Right Walking Stance* and execute a *High Long Fist Punch* with your Left fist. Perform in slow motion.

Previous   *Moves 11, 12 & 13*

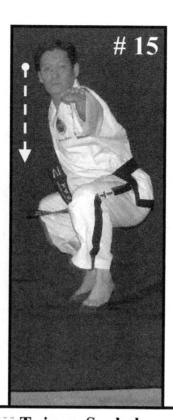

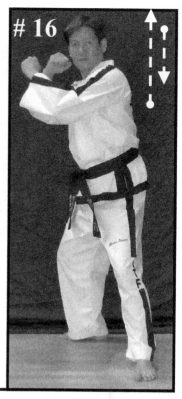

 **Kaunde Palmok
Daebi Makgi**
*Middle Forearm
Guarding Block*

**Twimyo Sonkal
Yop Taeragi**
*Flying Knifehand Side
Strike*

**Kyocha Joomok
Momchau Makgi**
X-Fist Checking Block

14. Slide backwards approximately half a stance with your Right leg, to form a *Right L-Stance* while executing a *Middle Forearm Guarding Block*.

15. Jump up and forwards approximately one stance length, executing a *(Flying) Knifehand Side Strike* whilst in the air, landing in a *Right L-Stance* and keeping the Knifehand Side Strike extended. *See moves 4a & 4 b.*

16. Shift backwards (approx. 6 inches) while maintaining the previous *Right L-Stance* and execute a X-*Fist Checking Block*.

Previous　　　　　　　　　　*Moves 15, 16 & 17*

Nopunde Bakuro Gutgi
High Outward Cross-Cut

**Sun Palkup
Naerjo Tulgi**
*Straight Elbow
Downward Thrust*

**Nopunde Dung
Joomok Taeragi**
High Back Fist Strike

17. Shift your Left foot to form *a Left Walking Stance* while executing a *High Outward Cross-Cut* with your Left hand.

18. Pull your Left foot back to form a *Right Rear Foot Stance* and execute a *Straight Elbow Downward Thrust* with your Left elbow.

19. Jump forwards a stance length into a *Right X-Stance*, executing a *High Back Fist Strike* with your Right fist.

Previous   *Moves 17, 18 & 19*

**Najunde Bandae
Bakuro Sonkal Makgi**
*Low Reverse Outward
Knifehand Block*

**Sonbadak Golcha
Makgi**
Palm Hooking Block

**Kaunde Ap
Joomok Jirugi**
Middle Forefist Punch

20. Move your Left foot backwards to form a *Right Walking Stance* while executing a *Low Reverse Outward Knifehand Block* with your Left hand.

21. Bring your Left foot in line with your right foot to form a *Parallel Stance* and execute a *Middle Palm Hooking Block* with your Right hand.

22. Maintain your stance and execute a *Middle Forefist Punch* with your Left fist.

Previous

Moves 20, 21 & 22

Sonkal Dung San Makgi
Reverse Knifehand W Block

**Sang Soopyong
Palkup Tulgi**
Twin Horizontal Elbow Thrust

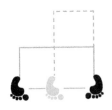

23. Move your Right foot out into a Sitting Stance while executing a *Reverse Knifehand W Block*.

24. Travelling to your right, move your Left foot in front of your right foot to form a *Right X-Stance* while executing a *Twin Horizontal Elbow Thrust*.

Previous

Moves 23 & 24

Sang Son Palmok Momchau Makgi
Twin Straight Forearm Checking Block

Ollyo Jirugi
Upward Punch

25. Continue travelling to your Right by moving your Right foot to form a *Sitting Stance* and execute a *Twin Straight Forearm Checking Block* with both forearms.

26. Continuing to your Right, move your Left foot in front of your Right foot to form a *Right X-Stance* while executing an *Upward Punch* with your Right fist, pulling your Left fist to your Right shoulder.

Previous   *Moves 25 & 26*

**Nopunde Bandae Dollyo
Goro Chagi**
High Reverse Hooking Kick

Nopunde Yop Cha Jirugi
High Side Piercing Kick

27. Spinning clockwise, execute a *High Reverse Hooking Kick* with your Right leg in the opposite direction to which you have been travelling i.e. 180 degrees.

28. Place your Right foot down (approximately a shoulder width from your Left foot) and execute a *High Side Piercing Kick* with your Left leg.

Previous   *Moves 27 & 28*

**Dung Joomok Naeryo
Taeragi**
Back Fist Downward Strike

Sonkal Dung San Makgi
Reverse Knifehand W Block

29. Lower your Left foot but do not place it on the ground. Instead, jump forwards (approximately one stance length in the same direction as the kick), landing in a *Left X-Stance* while executing a *Back Fist Downward Strike* with your Left fist.

30. Continuing in the current direction, move your Left foot to form a *Sitting Stance* and execute a *Reverse Knifehand W Block*.

Previous

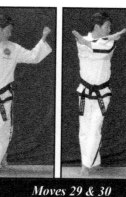

Moves 29 & 30

**Sang Soopyong
Palkup Tulgi**
Twin Horizontal Elbow Thrust

**Sang Son Palmok
Momchau Makgi**
Twin Straight Forearm Checking Block

Ollyo Jirugi
Upward Punch

31. Travelling to your Left, move your Right foot in front of your Left foot to form a *Left X-Stance* while executing a *Twin Horizontal Elbow Thrust*.

32. Continue travelling to your Left by moving your Left foot to form a *Sitting Stance* and execute a *Twin Straight Forearm Checking Block* with both forearms.

33. Continuing to your Left, move your Right foot in front of your Left foot to form a *Left X-Stance* while executing an *Upward Punch* with your Left fist, pulling your Right fist to your Left shoulder.

Previous   *Moves 31, 32 & 33*

Nopunde Bandae Dollyo Goro Chagi
High Reverse Hooking Kick

Nopunde Yop Cha Jirugi
High Side Piercing Kick

34. Spinning anti-clockwise, execute a *High Reverse Hooking Kick* with your Left leg in the opposite direction to which you have been travelling i.e. 180 degrees.

35. Lower your Left foot down (approximately a shoulder width in front) and execute a *High Side Piercing Kick* with your Right leg.

Previous   *Moves 34 & 35*

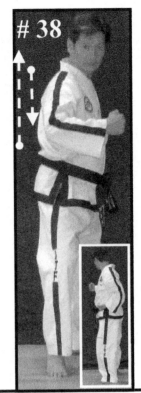

Dung Joomok Naeryo Taeragi
Back Fist Downward Strike

Kaunde Palmok Daebi Makgi
Middle Forearm Guarding Block

An Palmok Hori Makgi
Inner Forearm Waist Block

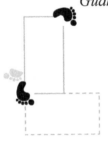

36. Lower your Right foot but do not place it on the ground. Instead, jump forwards (approximately one stance length in the same direction as the kick), landing in a *Right X-Stance* while executing a *Back Fist Downward Strike* with your Right fist.

37. Step 90 degrees backwards with your Left leg to form a *Left L-Stance* while executing a *Middle Forearm Guarding Block*.

38. Turn to face the opposite direction and move your Left foot round and behind you (anti-clockwise) to form a *Left Rear Foot Stance* executing an *Inner Forearm Waist Block* with your Right arm.

Previous

Moves 36, 37 & 38

**Nopunde Sonkal Yop
Taeragi**
High Knifehand Side Strike

**Kaunde Palmok
Daebi Makgi**
*Middle Forearm
Guarding Block*

**An Palmok
Hori Makgi**
*Inner Forearm
Waist Block*

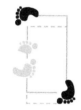

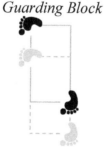

39. Move your Right foot backwards slightly (2 to 4 inches) and pivot 180 degrees anti-clockwise, stamping your Left foot as your form a *Right L-Stance* while executing a *High Knifehand Side Strike* with your Left hand.

40. Shift backwards (approx. 6 inches) while maintaining the previous *Right L-Stance* and execute a *Middle Forearm Guarding Block.*

41. Turn to face the opposite direction and move your Right foot round and behind you (clockwise) to form a *Right Rear Foot Stance* executing an *Inner Forearm Waist Block* with your Left arm.

Previous　　　　　　　　　　　　*Moves 39, 40 & 41*

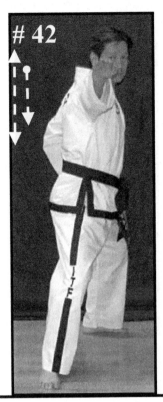

Nopunde Sonkal Yop Taeragi
High Knifehand Side Strike

Kaunde Palmok Daebi Makgi
Middle Forearm Guarding Block

Twio Dolmyo Chagi
Mid-Air Kick

42. Move your Left foot backwards slightly (2 to 4 inches) and pivot 180 degrees clockwise, stamping your Right foot as your form a *Left L-Stance* while executing a *High Knifehand Side Strike* with your Right hand.

43. Move your Right foot 180 degrees anti-clockwise to form a Right L-Stance while executing a *Middle Forearm Guarding Block* facing the previous direction.

44a. Jump forwards and execute a *Mid-Air Kick* with your Right leg, spinning in a clockwise direction.

Previous   *Moves 42, 43 & 44a*

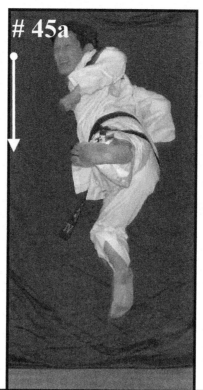

**Kaunde Sonkal
Daebi Makgi**
*Middle Knifehand
Guarding Block*

Twio Dolmyo Chagi
Mid Air Kick

**Kaunde Sonkal
Daebi Makgi**
*Middle Knifehand
Guarding Block*

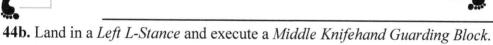

44b. Land in a *Left L-Stance* and execute a *Middle Knifehand Guarding Block*.

45a. Jump forwards and execute a *Mid Air Kick* with your Left leg, spinning in an anti-clockwise direction.

45b. Land in a *Right L-Stance* and execute a *Middle Knifehand Guarding Block*.

Previous

Moves 44b, 45a & 45b

Najunde Sonkal Dung Anuro Makgi
Low Reverse Knifehand Inward Block

Yop Palkup Tulgi
Side Elbow Thrust

Najunde Sonkal Dung Anuro Makgi
Low Reverse Knifehand Inward Block

46. Shift your Right foot to form a *Left Walking Stance* and execute a *Low Reverse Knifehand Inward Block* with your Right hand, pulling your Left fist to your Right shoulder.

47. Slide backwards approximately half a stance length into a *Left L-Stance*, while executing a *Side Elbow Thrust* with your Left elbow.

48. Shift your Left foot to form a *Right Walking Stance* and execute a *Low Reverse Knifehand Inward Block* with your Left hand, pulling your Right fist to your Left shoulder.

Previous | *Moves 46, 47 & 48*

49

Yop Palkup Tulgi
Side Elbow Thrust

Moosa Junbi Sogi 'A'
Warrior Ready Stance 'A'

49. Slide backwards approximately half a stance length into a *Right L-Stance*, while executing a *Side Elbow Thrust* with your Right elbow.

Return. Bring your Right foot back to the Ready Posture (*Warrior Ready Stance 'A'*)

Previous

Move 49 & return to ready posture

Tips For Yon-Gae Tul

1. The hardest part of the pattern to remember are moves #38 to #43 and which way to turn. To remember, think of them as counter-clockwise or clockwise or simply left and right.

2. Once you get moves #38 to #43 repetition is the only way to remember the sequence. Build and trust your muscle memory.

Ul-Ji

General Ul-Ji Moon Dok

을 지 틀

Ul-Ji is named after General Ul-Ji Moon Dok who successfully defended Korea against a Tang invasion force of nearly one million soldiers, led by Yang Je in 612 A.D. Ul-Ji, employing hit and run guerrilla tactics, was able to decimate a large percentage of the force. The diagram represents his surname. Ul-Ji has 42 movements which represent the author's age when he designed the pattern.

**Narani Sogi,
Kyocha Sondung**
Parallel Stance with X-Backhand

Sang Yop Joomok Soopyong Taeragi
Twin Side Fist Horizontal Strike

1. From *Parallel Stance with X-Backhand*, move your Left foot backwards to form a *Right Walking Stance* while executing *a Twin Side Fist Horizontal Strike*.

Hand Position

From the ready posture to move 1

 # 2

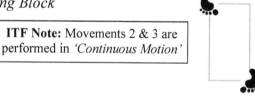

 # 3

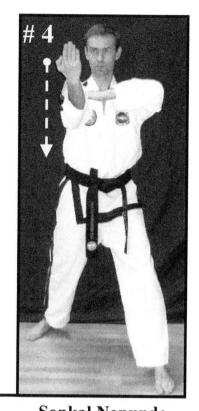

 # 4

**Kyocha Joomok
Najunde Noollo
Makgi**
*X-Fist Low
Pressing Block*

**Kyocha Sonkal
Chookyo Makgi**
X-Knifehand Rising Block

**Sonkal Nopunde
Bandae Ap Taeragi**
*Knifehand High Reverse
Front Strike*

ITF Note: Movements 2 & 3 are
performed in *'Continuous Motion'*

2. Move your Right foot backwards to form a *Left Walking Stance* while executing an *X-Fist Pressing Block*.

3. Maintain your stance and execute a *X-Knifehand Rising Block*.

4. Maintain your stance and execute a *Knifehand High Reverse Front Strike* with your Right hand, placing your Left palm on top of your Right elbow joint.

Previous

Moves 2, 3 & 4

Sondung Soopyong Taeragi
Backhand Horizontal Strike

Kaunde Bandal Chagi
Middle Crescent Kick

Ap Palkup Taeragi
Front Elbow Strike

5. Move your left foot 180 degrees anti-clockwise to your rear to form a *Sitting Stance*, while executing a *Backhand Horizontal Strike* with your Left hand.

6. Execute a *Middle Crescent Kick* to your Left palm with your Right leg.

7. Following the previous kick, lower your Right foot to form a *Sitting Stance* at 90 degrees anti-clockwise from the direction you were travelling while executing a *Right Front Elbow Strike* to your Left palm.

Previous   *Moves 5, 6 & 7*

Dwit Palkup Tulgi
Back Elbow Thrust

**Dung Joomok
Yop Dwit Taeragi**
Back Fist Side back Strike

**Sang Yop
Palkup Tulgi**
Twin Side Elbow Thrust

8. Maintain your stance and execute a *Back Elbow Thrust* with your Left elbow, placing your Right side fist on top of your Left fist. Remain facing forwards as you execute this move.

9. Maintain your stance and execute a *Back Fist Side Back Strike* with your Right fist, bringing your Left arm downwards in a similar motion to a *Low Forearm Block*.

10. Taking your weight on your Right foot, pivot 90 degrees anti-clockwise, bringing your Left foot to your Right foot to form a *Closed Stance* while executing a *Twin Side Elbow Thrust*.

Previous   *Moves 8, 9 & 10*

Kyocha Sogi
X-Stance

Kaunde Yop Cha Jirugi
Middle Side Piercing Kick

ITF Note: Movement 11 is
performed in *'Fast Motion'*

11. Move your Left foot across the front of your Right foot to form a *Right X-Stance* looking sharply to your Right, maintaining your hand positions as they were in move 10.

12. Execute a *Middle Side Piercing Kick* with your Right leg in the direction you are travelling, maintaining your hand positions as they were in moves 10 and 11.

Previous

Moves 11 & 12

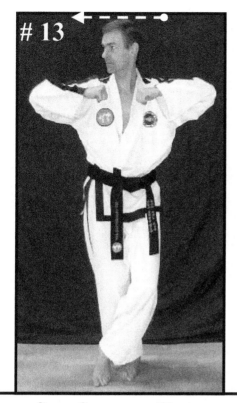

Sang Soopyong Yop Palkup Tulgi
Twin Horizontal Side Elbow Thrust

Soopyong Jirugi
Horizontal Punch

13. Following the previous kick lower your Right foot, then move your Left foot across the front of your Right foot to form a *Right X-Stance* while executing a *Twin Horizontal Side Elbow Thrust*.

14. Move your Right foot out to the side to form a *Sitting Stance* while executing a *Right Horizontal Punch*.

Previous

Moves 13 & 14

Sonkal Nopunde Ap Taeragi
Knifehand High Front Strike

Sang Sonkal Makgi
Twin Knifehand Block

15. Without moving your feet, rise up from your previous Sitting Stance while executing a *Knifehand High Front Strike* with your Right hand, bringing the back of your Left hand in front of your forehead.

16. Move your Left foot to form a *Right L-Stance*, facing 90 degrees anti-clockwise from your previous position while executing a *Twin Knifehand Block*.

Previous　　　　　　　*Moves 16 & 17*

Twio Dolmyo Chagi
Mid-Air Kick

Kaunde Doo Palmok Makgi
Middle Double Forearm Block

17. Jump up and spin anti-clockwise to execute a *Mid-Air Kick* with your Right leg.

18. Following the previous kick, land to form a *Right Walking Stance* while executing a *Middle Double Forearm Block*.

Previous   *Moves 18 & 19*

Moa Junbi Sogi 'B'
Closed Ready Stance 'B'

**Dung Joomok
Nopunde Yop Taeragi**
Back Fist High Side Strike

**Bandae Palmok
Chookyo Makgi**
Reverse Forearm Rising Block

19. Pivoting 90 degrees clockwise, bring your Left foot to your Right foot to form a *Closed Ready Stance 'B'*.

20. Jump forwards to form a *Right X-Stance* while executing a *Back Fist High Side Strike* with your Right hand, bringing your Left finger belly to the side of your Right fist.

21. Move your Left leg backwards to form a *Right Walking Stance*, while executing a *Reverse Forearm Rising Block* with your Left arm.

Previous

Moves 19, 20 & 21

Kaunde Ap Cha Busigi
Middle Front Snap Kick

**Nopunde Bandae
Ap Joomok Jirugi**
High Reverse Forefist Punch

Sun Sonkut Tulgi
Straight Fingertip Thrust

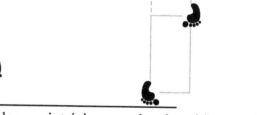

22. Execute a *Middle Front Snap Kick* with your Left leg, maintaining your hand positions as they were in move 21.

23. Following the previous kick, lower your Left foot in front to form a *Left Walking Stance* while executing a *High Reverse Forefist Punch* with your Right fist.

24. Move forwards to form a *Right Walking Stance* while executing a *Straight Fingertip Thrust* with your Right hand.

Previous — Moves 22, 23 & 24

Dung Joomok Nopunde Yop Taeragi
High Backfist Side Strike

Gunnon Junbi Sogi
Walking Ready Stance

Twimyo Nopi Chagi
Flying High Kick

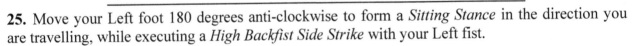

25. Move your Left foot 180 degrees anti-clockwise to form a *Sitting Stance* in the direction you are travelling, while executing a *High Backfist Side Strike* with your Left fist.

26. Move your right foot 270 degrees anti-clockwise to form a *Right Walking Ready Stance*.

27. Using a *double motion* (by raising your Left knee first) execute a *Flying High Kick* with your Right leg.

Previous   *Moves 25, 26 & 27*

Kyocha Sonkal Kaunde Makgi
X-Knifehand Middle Block

Kyocha Joomok Noollo Makgi
X-Fist Pressing Block

ITF Note: For ITF Students this is a *X-Knifehand Checking Block (*Kyocha Sonkal Momchau Makgi) and comes straight out from chest height.

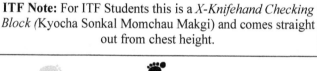

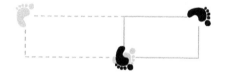

28. Following the previous kick, land to form a *Right Fixed Stance* while executing a *X-Knifehand Middle Block.*

29. Move your Left foot forwards to form a *Right L-Stance* while executing a *X-Fist Pressing Block.*

Previous   *Moves 28 & 29*

Kaunde Ap Cha Busigi /
Kaunde An Palmok Hechyo Makgi
*Middle Front Snap Kick /
Middle Inner Forearm Wedging Block*

Sang Sewo Jirugi
Twin Vertical Punch

30. Taking your weight on your Right leg, simultaneously execute a *Middle Front Snap Kick* with your Left leg and a *Middle Inner Forearm Wedging Block* with both arms.

31. Following the previous kick/combination, lower your Left foot in front to form a *Left Walking Stance* while executing a *Twin Vertical Punch*.

Previous   *Moves 30 & 31*

Sonkal Kaunde Yop Makgi / Sonbadak Miro Makgi
Middle Knifehand Outward Block / Middle Palm Pushing Block

Kaunde Bandae Ap Joomok Jirugi
Middle Reverse Forefist Punch

32. Move your Right foot forwards to form a *Right Fixed Stance* while simultaneously executing a *Middle Knifehand Outward Block* with your Right hand and a *Middle Palm Pushing Block* with your Left hand.

33. *Slide* forwards to form a *Right L-Stance* while executing a *Middle Forefist Reverse Punch* with your Left fist.

Previous

Moves 32 & 33

Dwiro Ibo Omgyo Didimyo Twigi
Backwards Double Step Jumping

Kaunde Palmok Daebi Makgi
Middle Forearm Guarding Block

> **Note:** The foot diagram shows the steps for 34a to 34c (from right to left)

34a. Keep facing the same direction and move your Left (front) foot backwards (beyond your Right foot), then move your Right foot backwards to form a *Right L-Stance*.

34b. Maintain your stance and jump backwards approximately one stance length.

34c. Following the jump, land in a *Right L-Stance* while executing a *Middle Forearm Guarding Block.*

- Perform all the above in one continuous motion -

Previous

Moves 34a, 34b & 34c

Kaunde Dollyo Chagi
Middle Turning Kick

35. Execute a Middle Turning Kick with your Right leg.

Previous   *Move 35*

Kaunde Dwit Cha Jirugi
Middle Back Piercing Kick

Kaunde Palmok
Daebi Makgi
Middle Forearm Guarding Block

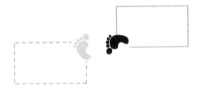

36. Following the previous kick, lower your Right foot in front then execute a *Middle Back Piercing Kick* with your Left leg.

37. Following the previous kick, lower your Left foot in front to form a *Right L-Stance*, while executing a *Middle Forearm Guarding Block*.

Previous   *Moves 36 & 37*

Sonbadak Ollyo Makgi
Palm Upward Block

An Palmok Dollimyo Makgi
Inner Forearm Circular Block

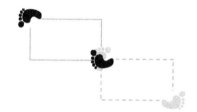

38. Move your Left foot backwards to form a *Left L-Stance* while executing a *Palm Upward Block* with your Right palm.

39. Taking your weight and pivoting on your Left foot, move your Right foot 180 degrees clockwise to form a *Right Walking Stance* while executing a *Middle Inner Forearm Circular Block* with your Left arm.

Previous   *Moves 38 & 39*

An Palmok Dollimyo Makgi
Inner Forearm Circular Block

Kaunde Ap Joomok Jirugi
Middle Forefist Punch

40. Pivot 135 degrees anti-clockwise on the balls of your feet to form a *Left Walking Stance* while executing a *Middle Inner Forearm Circular Block* with your Right arm.

41. Move your Left foot backwards to form a Sitting Stance while executing a *Left Middle Forefist Punch*.

Previous

Moves 40 & 41

Kaunde Ap Joomok Jirugi
Middle Forefist Punch

Narani Sogi,
Kyocha Sondung
Parallel Stance with X-Backhand

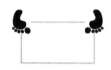

42. Maintain your stance and execute a *Right Middle Forefist Punch.*

Return. Bring your Left foot back to the Ready Posture (*Parallel Stance with X-Backhand*)

Previous

Move 49 & return to ready posture

Tips For Ul-Ji Tul

1. Ul-Ji is a fairly straight forward pattern, though the Mid-Air Kick (move #17) may require some extra practice.

2. Moves #11 and #34 (The step into X-Stance and the backwards jump) seem strange at first, but they will soon become familiar and natural with practice.

Moon-Moo
30th King Of The Silla Dynasty

Moon-Moo honours the 30th King of the Silla Dynasty. His body was buried near Dae Wang Am (Great King's Rock). According to his will, the body was placed in the sea *"where my soul shall forever defend my land against the Japanese"*. It is said that the Sok Gul Am (Stone cave) was built to guard his tomb. The Sok Gul Am is a fine example of the culture of the Silla Dynasty. Moon-Moo has 61 movements which symbolize the last two figures of 661 A.D. when Moon Moo came to the throne.

Narani Junbi Sogi
Parallel Ready Stance

Goburyo Junbi Sogi 'A'
Bending Ready Stance 'A'
(slow motion)

1. From *Parallel Ready Stance* turn to your Left, bringing your Left foot up to form a *Bending Ready Stance 'A'*. Perform in slow motion.

Note

For this chapter I have not reversed any of the main photographs to avoid confusion. All of the rear facing moves are repeated or have previously been performed in other patterns (so are not new to the student) so please refer to them should you need to.

Nopunde Yop Cha Jirugi
High Side Piercing Kick
(slow motion)

2. Execute a *High Side Piercing Kick* with your Left leg. Perform in slow motion.

From the ready posture to moves 1 & 2

Nopunde Yop Cha Jirugi
High Side Piercing Kick

Note: Movements 2 & 3 are performed as *'Double Kicks'*

Kaunde Opun Sonkut Tulgi
Middle Flat Fingertip Thrust

3. Following the previous kick, re-chamber and execute a *High Side Piercing Kick* with your Left leg. Perform in normal/fast motion.

4. Following the previous kick, lower your Left foot to form a *Sitting Stance* while executing a *Middle Flat Fingertip Thrust* with your Right hand.

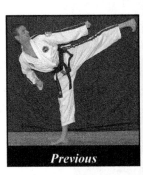

Previous

Moves 3 & 4

Nopunde Bandae Dollyo Goro Chagi
High Reverse Hooking Kick
(slow motion)

Sonkal Yop Taeragi
Knifehand Side Strike

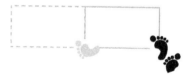

5. Taking your weight onto your Left leg, execute a *High Reverse Hooking Kick* with your Right Leg (Spinning clockwise). Perform in slow motion.

6. Following the previous kick, lower your Right foot and jump forwards to form a *Right X-Stance* while executing a *Knifehand Side Strike* with your Right hand.

Previous

Moves 5 & 6

Sonbadak Noollo Makgi
Palm Pressing Block

Sonbadak Noollo Makgi
Palm Pressing Block

7. Travelling in the opposite direction, move your Left foot to form a *Left Walking Stance* while executing a *Right Palm Pressing Block*. Perform at normal speed.

8. Move your Right foot to form a *Right Walking Stance* while executing a *Left Palm Pressing Block*. Perform at normal speed.

Previous

Moves 7 & 8

**Waebal Sogi,
Nopunde/Najunde Sonkal Yop Makgi**
One-Leg Stance, High/Low Knifehand Side Block
(slow motion)

Goburyo Junbi Sogi 'A'
Bending Ready Stance 'A'
(slow motion)

9. Pivoting 90 degrees anti-clockwise, bring your Left foot in and up to form a *Right One-Leg Stance* while simultaneously executing a *High Knifehand Side Block* with your Left hand and a *Low Knifehand Side Block* with your Right Hand. Perform in slow motion.

10. Lower your Left foot to the floor and raise your Right foot to form a *Bending Ready Stance 'A'*, facing 90 degrees clockwise. Perform in slow motion.

Previous   *Moves 9 & 10*

Nopunde Yop Cha Jirugi
High Side Piercing Kick
(slow motion)

11. Execute a *High Side Piercing Kick* with your Right leg. Perform in slow motion.

Previous   *Move 11*

Nopunde Yop Cha Jirugi
High Side Piercing Kick

Kaunde Opun Sonkut Tulgi
Middle Flat Fingertip Thrust

Note: Movements 11 & 12 are performed as *'Double Kicks'*

 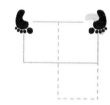

12. Following the previous kick, re-chamber and execute a *High Side Piercing Kick* with your Right leg. Perform in normal/fast motion.

13. Following the previous kick, lower your Right foot to form a *Sitting Stance* while executing a *Middle Flat Fingertip Thrust* with your Left hand.

Previous   *Moves 12 & 13*

Nopunde Bandae Dollyo Goro Chagi
High Reverse Hooking Kick
(slow motion)

Sonkal Yop Taeragi
Knifehand Side Strike

14. Taking your weight onto your Right leg, execute a *High Reverse Hooking Kick* with your Left Leg (Spinning anti-clockwise). Perform in slow motion.

15. Following the previous kick, lower your Left foot and jump forwards to form a *Left X-Stance* while executing a *Knifehand Side Strike* with your Left hand.

Previous

Moves 14 & 15

Sonbadak Noollo Makgi
Palm Pressing Block

Sonbadak Noollo Makgi
Palm Pressing Block

16. Travelling in the opposite direction, move your Right foot to form a *Right Walking Stance* while executing a *Left Palm Pressing Block*. Perform at normal speed.

17. Move your Left foot to form a *Left Walking Stance* while executing a *Right Palm Pressing Block*. Perform at normal speed.

Previous

Moves 16 & 17

Waebal Sogi, Nopunde/ Najunde Sonkal Yop Makgi
One-Leg Stance, High/Low Knifehand Side Block
(slow motion)

Goburyo Junbi Sogi 'B'
Bending Ready Stance 'B'

18. Pivoting 90 degrees clockwise, bring your Right foot in and up to form a *Left One-Leg Stance* while simultaneously executing a *High Knifehand Side Block* with your Right and a *Low Knifehand Side Block* with your Left Hand. Perform in slow motion.

19. Relax from your previous stance but do not allow your foot to touch the floor, then sharply chamber into a *Left Bending Ready Stance 'B'*, looking over your Right shoulder.

Previous

Moves 18 & 19

Nopunde Dwitcha Jirugi
High Back Piercing Kick
(Slow Motion)

**Kaunde Bandae
Ap Joomok Jirugi**
Middle Reverse Forefist Punch

20. Execute a *Middle Back Piercing Kick* with your Right leg. Perform in slow motion.

21. Following the previous kick, lower your Right foot behind to form a *Left Walking Stance* while executing a *Middle Reverse Forefist Punch* with your Right fist.

Previous   *Moves 20 & 21*

Goburyo Junbi Sogi 'B'
Bending Ready Stance 'B'

Nopunde Dwitcha Jirugi
High Back Piercing Kick
(Slow Motion)

22. Withdraw your Left foot to form a *Right Bending Ready Stance 'B'*, looking over your Left shoulder.

23. Execute a *High Back Piercing Kick* with your Left leg. Perform in slow motion.

Previous   *Moves 22 & 23*

**Kaunde Bandae
Ap Joomok Jirugi**
*Middle Reverse Forefist
Punch*

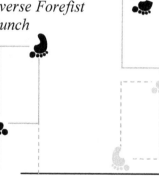

**Sonbadak Naeryo
Makgi**
*Palm Downward
Block*

**Kaunde Yop Ap Cha
Busigi**
Middle Side Front Snap Kick

24. Following the previous kick, lower your Left foot behind to form a *Right Walking Stance* while executing a *Middle Reverse Forefist Punch* with your Left fist.

25. *Slide* backwards (but remain facing the current direction) to form a *Right Rear Foot Stance* while executing a *Left Palm Downward Block*.

26. Taking your weight on your Right foot, execute a *Middle Side Front Snap Kick* with your Left leg, maintaining the hand positions as they were in move25.

Previous

Moves 24, 25 & 26

 # 27

 # 28 **# 29**

Yop Joomok Kaunde Yop Taeragi
Side-Fist Middle Side Strike

Sonbadak Duro Makgi
Palm Scooping Block

Kaunde Ap Joomok Jirugi
Middle Forefist Punch

ITF Note: Movements 28 & 29 are performed in *'Connecting Motion'*

27. Following the previous kick, lower your Left foot in front, but in-line with your Right foot (approx. half a shoulder width), then stamp your Right foot into a *Sitting Stance* in the opposite direction, executing a *Right Side-Fist Middle Side Strike*.

28. Slide in the direction of your previous strike while maintaining your *Sitting Stance* and execute a *Palm Scooping Block* with your Left hand.

29. Maintain your stance and execute a *Middle Forefist Punch* with your Right fist.

Previous

Moves 27, 28 & 29

Najunde Sonkal Yop Makgi
Low Knifehand Side Block

Durokamyo Kaunde Yop Cha Milgi
Skipping Middle Side Pushing Kick

Nopunde Bandae Dollyo Chagi
High Reverse Turning Kick

30. Maintain your stance and execute a *Low Knifehand Side Block* with your Left hand.

31. Skipping to your Right, so your Left foot replaces your Right foot, execute a *Middle Side Pushing Kick* with your Right leg.

32. Following the previous kick, lower your Right foot and execute a *High Reverse Turning Kick* with your Left leg in the current direction you are travelling.

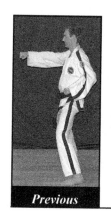

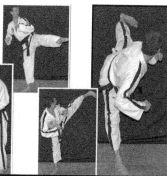

Previous

Moves 30, 31 & 32

Nopunde Sonkal Yop Makgi
High Knifehand Side Block

Sonbadak Naeryo Makgi
Palm Downward Block

Kaunde Yop Ap Cha Busigi
Middle Side Front Snap Kick

33. Following the previous kick, lower your Left leg to form a *Left Walking Stance* while executing a *High Knifehand Side Block* with your Left hand.

34. Slide backwards (but remain facing the current direction) to form a *Left Rear Foot Stance* while executing a *Right Palm Downward Block*.

35. Taking your weight on your Left foot, execute a *Middle Side Front Snap Kick* with your Right leg, maintaining your hand positions as they were in move 34.

Previous   *Moves 33, 34 & 35*

Yop Joomok Kaunde Yop Taeragi
Side-Fist Middle Side Strike

Sonbadak Duro Makgi
Palm Scooping Block

Ap Joomok Jirugi
Forefist Punch

ITF Note: Movements 37 & 38 are performed in *'Connecting Motion'*

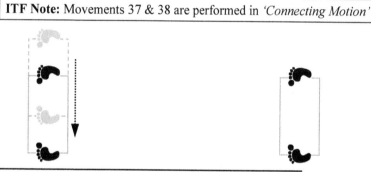
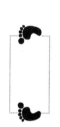

36. Following the previous kick, lower your Right foot in front, but in-line with your Left foot (approx. half a shoulder width), then stamp your Left foot into a *Sitting Stance* in the opposite direction while executing a *Left Middle Side-Fist Side Strike*.

37. Maintain your *Sitting Stance* and slide in the direction of your previous while executing a *Palm Scooping Block* with your Right hand.

38. Maintain your stance and execute a *Middle Forefist Punch* with your Left fist.

Previous   *Moves 36, 37 & 38*

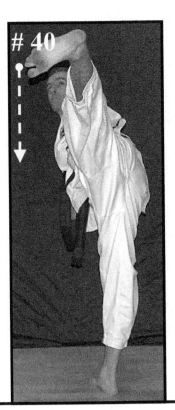
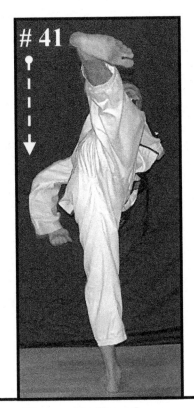

Najunde Sonkal Yop Makgi
Low Knifehand Side Block

Durokamyo Kaunde Yop Cha Milgi
Skipping Middle Side Pushing Kick

Nopunde Bandae Dollyo Chagi
High Reverse Turning Kick

39. Maintain your stance and execute a *Low Knifehand Side Block* with your Right hand.

40. Skipping to your Left so your Right foot replaces your Left foot and execute a *Middle Side Pushing Kick* with your Left leg.

41. Following the previous kick, lower your Left foot and execute a *High Reverse Turning Kick* with your Right leg in the current direction you are travelling.

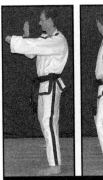

Previous   *Moves 39, 40 & 41*

**Nopunde Sonkal
Yop Makgi**
High Knifehand Side Block

Nopunde Bituro Chagi
High Twisting Kick

**Dung Joomok Taeragi /
Najunde Bakat
Palmok Makgi**
*Back Fist Strike / Low Outer
Forearm Block*

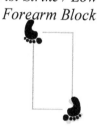

42. Following the previous kick, lower your Right leg to form a *Right Walking Stance* while executing a *High Knifehand Side Block* with your Right hand.

43. Move your rear (Left) foot past your front (Right) foot and execute a *High Twisting Kick* with your Right leg.

44. Following the previous kick, lower your Right foot behind to form a *Left Walking Stance* while simultaneously executing a *Back Fist Strike* with your Right fist and a *Low Outer Forearm Block* with your Left arm.

Previous   *Moves 42, 43 & 44*

**Dung Joomok
Ap Taeragi**
Backfist Front Strike

Nopunde Bituro Chagi
High Twisting Kick

**Dung Joomok Taeragi /
Najunde Bakat
Palmok Makgi**
*Back Fist Strike / Low Outer
Forearm Block*

45. Maintaining your stance slide backwards 6 inches and execute a *Backfist Front Strike* with your Right fist, bringing your Left fist underneath your Right elbow.

46. Move your rear (Right) foot past your front (Left) foot and execute a *High Twisting Kick* with your Left leg.

47. Following the previous kick, lower your Left foot behind to form a *Right Walking Stance* while simultaneously executing a *Back Fist Strike* with your Left fist and a *Low Outer Forearm Block* with your Right arm.

Previous | *Moves 45, 46 & 47*

48

49a

49b

**Dung Joomok
Ap Taeragi**
Backfist Front Strike

Suroh Chagi
Sweeping Kick

**Kaunde Palmok
Daebi Makgi**
*Middle Forearm
Guarding Block*

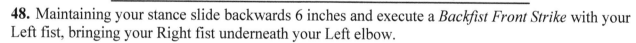

48. Maintaining your stance slide backwards 6 inches and execute a *Backfist Front Strike* with your Left fist, bringing your Right fist underneath your Left elbow.

49a. Keep your arms in their previous position and execute a *Sweeping Kick* with your Left foot.

49b. Following the previous Sweeping Kick, lower your Left foot to form a *Right L-Stance* while executing a *Middle Forearm Guarding Block*.

Previous

Moves 48, 49a & 49b

Yop Cha Momchugi
Side Checking Kick

Kaunde Yop Cha Tulgi
Middle Side Thrusting Kick

Sonkal Yop Taeragi
Knifehand Side Strike

ITF Note: Movements 50a & 50b are performed as *'Consecutive Kicks'*

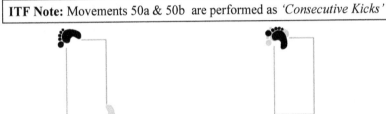

50a. Taking your weight on your Right foot, execute a *Side Checking Kick* with your Left (front) leg.

50b. Without placing your Left foot down, re-chamber and execute a *Middle Side Thrusting Kick* with your Left leg.

51. Following the previous kick, lower your Left foot in front to form a *Right L-Stance* while executing a *Knifehand Side Strike* with your Left hand.

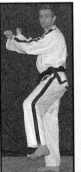

Previous · *Moves 50a, 50b & 51*

Suroh Chagi
Sweeping Kick

Kaunde Palmok Daebi Makgi
Middle Forearm Guarding Block

Yop Cha Momchugi
Side Checking Kick

52a. Keep your arms in their previous position and execute a *Sweeping Kick* with your Right foot.

52b. Following the previous Sweeping Kick, lower your Right foot to form a *Left L-Stance* while executing a *Middle Forearm Guarding Block*.

53a. Take your weight on your Left foot and execute a *Side Checking Kick* with your Right (front) leg.

Previous — *Moves 52a, 52b & 53*

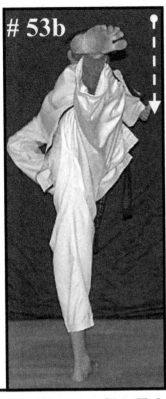

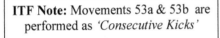

Kaunde Yop Cha Tulgi
Middle Side Thrusting Kick

Sonkal Yop Taeragi
Knifehand Side Strike

Kaunde Bandae Ap Joomok Jirugi
Middle Reverse Forefist Punch

ITF Note: Movements 53a & 53b are performed as *'Consecutive Kicks'*

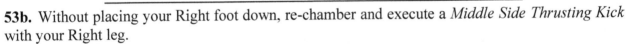

53b. Without placing your Right foot down, re-chamber and execute a *Middle Side Thrusting Kick* with your Right leg.

54. Following the previous kick, lower your Right foot in front to form a *Left L-Stance* while executing a *Knifehand Side Strike* with your Right hand.

55. Move your Right foot backwards (but remain facing forwards), then pivot 180 degrees anti-clockwise on your Right foot, moving your Left foot around to form a *Left Walking Stance* while executing a *Middle Reverse Forefist Punch* with your Right fist.

Previous — *Moves 53b, 54 & 55*

**Kyocha Sogi,
Najunde Jirugi**
X-Stance, Low Punch

**Kyocha Sogi,
Najunde Jirugi**
X-Stance, Low Punch

Twio Dolmyo Chagi
Mid-Air Kick

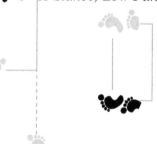

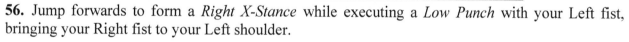

56. Jump forwards to form a *Right X-Stance* while executing a *Low Punch* with your Left fist, bringing your Right fist to your Left shoulder.

57. Jump in the opposite direction (180 degrees) to form a *Left X-Stance* while executing a *Low Punch* with your Right fist, bringing your Left fist to your Right shoulder.

58. From your previous X-Stance, jump up, spinning clockwise and execute a *Mid-Air Kick* with your Right leg.

Previous　　　　　　　　　　　　　　　*Moves 56, 57 & 58*

**Kaunde Sonkal
Daebi Makgi**
*Middle Knifehand
Guarding Block*

**Bandalson Bandae
Chookyo Makgi**
*Arc-Hand
Reverse Rising Block*

**Nopunde Ap
Joomok Jirugi**
High Forefist Punch

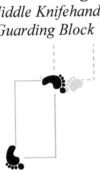

59. Following the previous kick, land in a Left L-Stance while executing a *Middle Knifehand Guarding Block.*

60. Move your Right foot backwards past your Left foot, then move your Left foot backwards to form a *Right Walking Stance* (facing forwards throughout), while executing an *Arc-Hand Reverse Rising Block* with your Left hand.

61. Maintain your stance and execute a *High Forefist Punch* with your Right fist.

Previous

Moves 59, 60 & 61

Narani Junbi Sogi
Parallel Ready Stance

Return. Upon completion of the pattern, bring your right foot backwards to *Parallel Ready Stance*.

Previous   *Return To Ready Posture*

Tips For Moon-Moo Tul

1. This pattern has a lot of slow motion kicking techniques in it, so extra leg strength training may prove useful so the techniques can be executed both slowly and with accuracy.

2. The Palm Pressing Blocks (moves #7 to #8 and #16 to #17) are perform individually, with slight pauses between them rather than the *'walking'* motion used in pattern Choi-Yong.

3. The Side Checking Kicks (moves #50a and #53a) are executed in an almost *'soft'* way, rather than fast and sharp and the knee remains slightly bent on the kicking leg.

Sun-Duk

Queen Sun Duk

선 덕 형

Sun-Duk is named after Queen Sun Duk of the Silla dynasty in the year 668 A.D. Queen Sun Duk was known for bringing martial art from China to Korea. Sun-Duk has 68 movements which refer to the year 668 A.D. and the diagram represents 'Lady'.

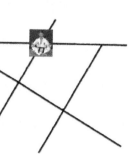

Ready Posture

 # 1a

Yang Ban Da Ri
Sitting Cross Legged
(Fists On Top Of Knees)

Nopunde Yop Cha Jirugi
High Side Piercing Kick

Note: *For this chapter there are so many 30° angles involved that I have not reversed any of the main photographs to avoid confusion. Many of the rear facing moves are repeated, so please refer to them if the technique is new to you and most others can be found in other patterns for further reference.*

1a. From the ready posture of *Sitting Cross Legged with fists on top of knees,* place your hands to your Left, 30 degrees behind you while executing a *Right High Side Piercing Kick* (from the floor) at a 30 degrees angle in front.

From the ready posture to moves 1a & 1b

Nopunde Dollyo Goro Chagi
High Hooking Kick

Note: Movements 1a & 1b are performed in *'Connecting Motion'*

Ban Gunnon Sogi,
Nopunde Jirugi / Bandalson Naeryo
Half Walking Stance,
High Punch / Arc-Hand Pressing

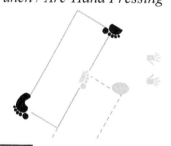

1b. Without placing your foot down, consecutively execute a *High Hooking Kick* with your Right leg at the same 30 degree angle.

2. Following the previous kick, lower your foot to form a *Half Walking Stance* while executing a *High Obverse Punch* with Right fist, pressing your *Left Arc-Hand to the floor*.

Previous

Move 2

Sonbadak Noollo Makgi
Palm Pressing Block
(Slow Motion)

Kyocha Joomok Chookyo Makgi
X-Fist Rising Block
(Slow Motion)

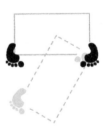

3. Bring your Left foot half way towards your Right foot. Rise up before sliding your Left foot backwards to form a *Right Walking Stance* while executing a *Left Palm Pressing Block*. Maintain the 30 degree angle and perform in slow motion.

4. Bring your Right foot towards your Left foot, then move your Right foot sideways to form a *Sitting Stance* facing straight forwards, while executing an *X-Fist Rising Block*. Perform in slow motion.

Previous   *Moves 3 & 4*

San Makgi
W Block

Kaunde Mikulmyo Yop Cha Jirugi
Middle Sliding Side Piercing Kick

5. Moving to your Right, pivot 180 degrees clockwise, stamping your Left foot to form a *Sitting Stance* while executing a *W Block*.

6a. Taking your weight on your Right foot, execute a *Middle Sliding Side Piercing Kick* with your Left leg.

Previous

Moves 5 & 6a

Sonkal Nopunde Bakuro Makgi / Sonbadak Miro Makgi
Middle Knifehand Outward Block / Middle Palm Pushing Block

San Makgi
W Block

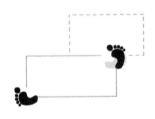

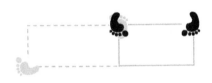

6b. Following the previous kick, lower your Left foot to form a *Left Fixed Stance* while simultaneously executing a *Left Middle Knifehand Outward Block* and *Right Middle Palm Pushing Block*.

7. Pivot 180 degrees clockwise in the opposite direction, stamping your Left foot to form a *Sitting Stance* while executing a *W Block*.

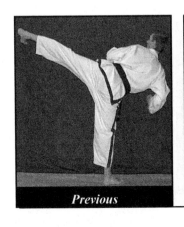

Previous   *Moves 6b & 7*

Kaunde Mikulmyo Yop Cha Jirugi
Middle Sliding Side Piercing Kick

**Sonkal Nopunde Bakuro Makgi /
Sonbadak Miro Makgi**
*Middle Knifehand Outward Block /
Middle Palm Pushing Block*

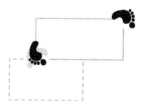

8a. Taking your weight on your Right foot, execute a *Middle Sliding Side Piercing Kick* with your Left leg.

8b. Following the previous kick, lower your Left foot to form a *Left Fixed Stance*, while simultaneously executing a *Left Middle Knifehand Outward Block* and *Right Middle Palm Pushing Block*.

Previous

Moves 8a & 8b

Najunde Palmok Ap Makgi
Low Forearm Front Block

Sang Bakat Palmok Narani Ap Makgi
Twin Outer Forearm Parallel Front Block

9. Move your Right foot in front of your Right foot to form a *Left X-Stance*, while executing a *Low Forearm Front Block* with your Left arm, bringing your Right fingerbelly to the side of your Left fist.

10. Move your Left foot sideways to form a *Sitting Stance* facing straight forwards, while executing a *Twin Outer Forearm Parallel Front Block* with both arms.

Previous

Moves 9 & 10

Sang Dwijibo Jirugi
Twin Upset Punch

Twimyo Ap Cha Busigi
Flying Front Snap Kick

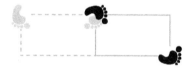

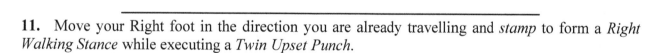

11. Move your Right foot in the direction you are already travelling and *stamp* to form a *Right Walking Stance* while executing a *Twin Upset Punch*.

12a. Jump forwards executing a *Right Flying Front Snap Kick*, using double (bicycle) motion, by raising your Left knee prior to kicking with your Right leg.

Previous   *Moves 11 & 12a*

Kyocha Sonkal Momchau Makgi
X-Knifehand Checking Block

Kaunde Ap Joomok Jirugi
Middle Forefist Punch

12b. Following the previous flying kick, land in a *Left L-Stance* while executing a *X-Knifehand Checking Block*.

13. Move your Left foot forwards and *slide* into a *Left Fixed Stance* while executing a *Middle Obverse Forefist Punch* with your Left fist.

Previous   *Moves 12b & 13*

Nopunde Dollyo Chagi
High Turning Kick

Twimyo Ap Cha Busigi
Flying Front Snap Kick

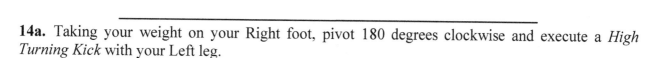

14a. Taking your weight on your Right foot, pivot 180 degrees clockwise and execute a *High Turning Kick* with your Left leg.

14b. Following the previous kick, lower your Left foot in front then jump forwards executing a *Left Flying Front Snap Kick*, using double (bicycle) motion by raising your Right knee prior to kicking with your Left leg.

Previous

Moves 14a & 14b

Kyocha Joomok Noollo Makgi
X-Fist Pressing Block

Nopunde Bandae Dollyo Chagi
High Reverse Turning Kick

15. Following the previous flying kick, land in a *Left Walking Stance* while executing a *X-Fist Pressing Block.*

16. Take your weight onto your Left leg and pivot 210 degrees clockwise, then execute a *High Reverse Turning Kick* at a 30 degree angle (along the vertical angled line in the pattern diagram).

Previous   *Moves 15 & 16*

Twimyo Yop Cha Jirugi
Flying Side Piercing Kick

Doo Sonbadak Ollyo Makgi
Double Palm Upward Block

**Doo Bandalson
Nopunde Makgi**
*Double Arc-Hand
High Block*

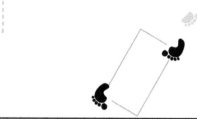

17. Following the previous kick, lower your Right foot in front and immediately execute a *Flying Side Piercing Kick* with your Right leg from a *twin foot take off*, maintaining the 30 angle you are currently travelling at.

18. Land from the previous flying kick in a *Right Walking Stance* while executing a *Double Palm Upward Block*, maintaining the 30 angle you are currently travelling at.

19. Move forwards (maintaining the 30 angle) to form a *Left Walking Stance* while executing a *Double Arc-Hand High Block* to your Right side.

Previous   *Moves 17, 18 & 19*

Sondung Bakuro Taeragi
Back-Hand Outward Strike

Nopunde Anuro Bandal Chagi
High Inside Crescent Kick

20. Move forwards with your Right foot in a *stamping* motion to form a *Left L-Stance* while executing a *Back-Hand Outward Strike* with your Right hand. Maintain the 30 angle you are currently travelling at.

21. While maintaining the 30 angle you are currently travelling at, execute a *High Inside Crescent Kick* to your Right Palm with your Left leg.

Previous *Moves 20 & 21*

**Twimyo Dolmyo
Anuro Bandal Chagi**
Flying Mid-Air Inside Crescent Kick

Sonkal Yop Taeragi
Knifehand Side Strike

**Sonbadak Noollo
Makgi**
Palm Pressing Block

22. Following the previous kick maintain the 30 angle you are travelling at and lower your Left foot in front. Execute a *Flying Mid-Air Inside Crescent Kick*, by raising your Right knee as you spin 180 degrees clockwise before executing the kick with your Left leg.

23. Following the previous flying kick, land to form a *Left X-Stance* (maintaining the 30 angle) while executing a *Knifehand Side Strike* with your Left hand.

24. Pivoting 180 degrees clockwise on your Left foot, move your Right foot forwards to form a *Right Walking Stance* while executing a *Left Palm Pressing Block*, while maintaining the 30 degree angle but now in the opposite direction.

Previous   *Moves 22, 23 & 24*

Sonbadak Noollo Makgi
Palm Pressing Block

Kaunde Ap Cha Busigi
Middle Front Snap Kick

Kaunde Bandae Ap Joomok Jirugi
Middle Reverse Forefist Punch

Note: Movements 24 & 25 are performed in *'Continuous Motion'*

25. Move your Left foot forwards to form a *Left Walking Stance* while executing a *Right Palm Pressing Block*, maintaining the 30 degree angle you are currently travelling..

26. Execute a *Middle Front Snap Kick* with your Right leg at the same 30 degree angle.

27. Following the kick, lower your Right foot to form a *Right Walking Stance* while executing a *Middle Reverse Forefist Punch* with your Left hand.

Previous   *Moves 25, 26 & 27*

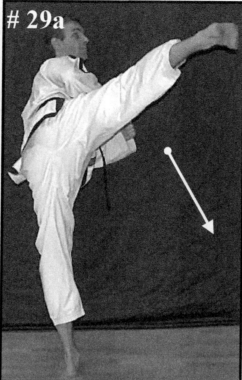

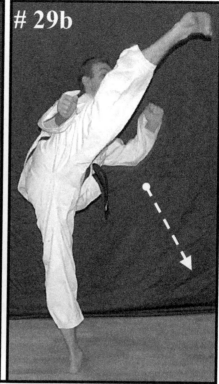

Sang Sonbadak
Noollo Makgi
Twin Palm
Pressing Block

Kaunde Dollyo Chagi
Middle Turning Kick
(Slow Motion)

Nopunde Dollyo Chagi
High Turning Kick
(Slow Motion)

Note: Movements 29a & 29b are performed in *'Continuous Slow Motion'* with 29c performed in *Continuous Fast Motion*

28. While travelling at the same 30 degree angle, bring your Left foot forwards to form a *Right Rear Foot Stance* while executing a *Twin Palm Pressing Block*.

29a. Execute a *Middle Turning Kick* 90 degrees to your Right. Perform in slow motion.

29b. Without placing your Right foot down, re-chamber and execute a *High Turning Kick* (in the same direction). Perform in slow motion.

Previous

Moves 28, 29a & 29b

Nopunde Goro Chagi
High Hooking Kick
(Fast Motion)

Twimyo Goro Chagi
Flying Hooking Kick

29c. Without placing your Right foot down, re-chamber and execute a *High Hooking Kick* (in the same direction). Perform in normal/fast motion.

30. Following the previous kick, place your Right foot down in front of you, then jump forwards (with a twin foot take off) and execute a *Flying Hooking Kick* with your Right leg.

Previous   *Moves 29c & 30*

 # 31

 # 32a

Kaunde Palmok Daebi Makgi
Middle Forearm Guarding Block

Ap Cha Milgi
Front Pushing Kick

31. Following the previous jumping kick, land to form a *Left L-Stance* while executing a *Middle Forearm Guarding Block*. You are now travelling at 30 degrees again, but to the opposite side than before.

32a. While *Sliding* forwards, execute a *Front Pushing Kick* with your Left leg at the 30 degree angle you are travelling at.

Previous

Moves 31 & 32a

**Kaunde Sonkal
Daebi Makgi**
*Middle Knifehand
Guarding Block*

**Pihamyo Twimyo
Ap Cha Busigi**
Dodging Flying Front Snap Kick

**Kaunde Palmok
Daebi Makgi**
*Middle Forearm
Guarding Block*

32b. Following the previous kick, lower your Left foot to form a *Right L-Stance* while executing a *Middle Knifehand Guarding Block* at the same 30 degree angle.

33. Using a twin foot take off, jump backwards and execute a *Dodging Flying Front Snap Kick* with your Right leg.

34. Following the previous jumping kick, land to form a *Left Rear Foot Stance* while executing a *Middle Forearm Guarding Block* at the same 30 degree angle.

Previous

Moves 32b, 33 & 34

Step Backwards

Sonbadak Ollyo Makgi
Palm Upward Block

Kaunde Baro
Ap Joomok Jirugi
Middle Obverse Forefist Punch

35a & b. Take a step backwards along the 30 degree angle, first moving your Right foot back, then moving your Left foot back to form a *Left L-Stance* while executing a *Palm Upward Block* with your Right palm.

36. *Slide* forwards maintaining both your *Left L-Stance* and the 30 degree angle you are facing, while executing a *Middle Obverse Forefist Punch* with your Left fist.

Previous

Moves 35a, 35b & 36

Dollimyo Makgi
Circular Block

Nopunde Baro Ap Joomok Jirugi
High Obverse Forefist Punch

37a. Take your weight on your Right foot and pivot 180 degrees anti-clockwise, moving your Left foot to form a *Left Walking Stance* while executing an *Inner Forearm Circular Block* with your Right arm.

37b. Maintain your stance and execute a *High Obverse Forefist Punch* with your Left fist.

Previous

Moves 37a & 37b

Kaunde Ap Cha Busigi
Middle Front Snap Kick

Nopunde Yop Cha Jirugi
High Side Piercing Kick

38. Maintain the current direction and execute a *Middle Front Snap K*ick with your Right leg.

39a. Following the previous kick, lower your Right foot in front then execute a *High Side Piercing Kick* with your Left leg in the same direction.

Previous

Moves 38 & 39a

Kaunde Sonkal Daebi Makgi
Middle Knifehand Guarding Block

Nopunde Bituro Chagi
High Twisting Kick

39b. Following the previous kick, lower your Left foot as you pivot 90 degrees clockwise on your Right foot, and place your Left foot behind you to form a *Left L-Stance* while executing a *Middle Knifehand Guarding Block*. You are now facing approximately North-East at a 30 degree angle.

40a & b. Move your Left foot forwards one step, then execute a *High Twisting Kick* with your Right leg.

Previous

Moves 39b, 40a & 40b

Twimyo Kaunde Bituro Chagi
Flying Middle Twisting Kick

**Nopunde Baro
Ap Joomok Jirugi**
High Obverse Forefist Punch

41a. Following the previous kick lower your Right foot in front, then execute a *Flying Middle Twisting Kick* in double (bicycle) motion. Raise your Left knee as you jump and kick with your Right leg.

41b. Following the previous flying kick, land to form a *Right Walking Stance*, maintaining the previous 30 degree angle and execute a *High Obverse Forefist Punch* with your Right fist.

Previous

Moves 41a & 41b

42a

42b

42c

43a

Double Step
Forwards

Nopunde Bituro Chagi
High Twisting Kick

**Twimyo Kaunde
Bituro Chagi**
Flying Middle Twisting Kick

42a, b & c. Perform a *double stepping movement* first by moving your Left foot forwards, followed by moving your Right foot forwards before executing a *High Twisting Kick* with your Left leg.

43a. Following the previous kick, lower your Left foot in front then execute a *Flying Middle Twisting Kick* in double (bicycle) motion. Raising your Right knee as you jump to kick with your Left leg.

Previous · Moves 42a, 42b, 42c & 43a

Nopunde Baro Ap Joomok Jirugi
High Obverse Forefist Punch

Kaunde Bakuro Sewo Cha Momchugi
Middle Outward Vertical Checking Kick

43b. Following the previous kick, land to form a *Left Walking Stance*, maintaining previous 30 degree angle and execute a *High Obverse Forefist Punch* with your Left fist.

44a. Taking your weight on your Left leg, pivot 330 degrees clockwise while executing a *Middle Outward Vertical Checking Kick* with your Right leg.

Previous   *Moves 43b & 44a*

Nopunde Dollyo Chagi
High Turning Kick

Nopunde Bakuro Gutgi
High Outward Cross-Cut

Note: Movements 44a & 44b are performed as *'Consecutive Kicks'*

44b. Without placing your Right foot down, re-chamber and execute a *High Turning Kick* with your Right leg.

44c. Following the previous kick, lower your Right foot in front to form a *Right Walking Stance* while executing a *High Outward Cross-Cut* with your Right fingertips.

Previous   *Moves 71, 72 & return to Ready Stance*

Kaunde Bakuro Sewo Cha Momchugi
Middle Outward Vertical Checking Kick

Nopunde Yop Cha Tulgi
High Side Thrusting Kick

Note: Movements 45a & 45b are performed as *'Consecutive Kicks'*

45a. Travelling in the current direction execute a *Middle Outward Vertical Checking Kick* with your Left leg.

45b. Without placing your Right foot down, re-chamber and execute a *High Side Thrusting Kick* with your Left leg.

Previous   *Moves 45a & 54b*

Nopunde Bakuro Gutgi
High Outward Cross-Cut

**Joongi Joomok Kaunde
Dwijibo Jirugi**
Middle Knuckle Fist Upset Punch

45c. Following the previous kick, lower your Left foot in front to form a *Left Walking Stance* while executing a *High Outward Cross-Cut* with your Left fingertips.

46. Move your Right foot forwards to form a *Left L-Stance* while executing a *Middle Knuckle Fist Upset Punch* with your Left fist, pulling your Right Side Fist to your Left shoulder.

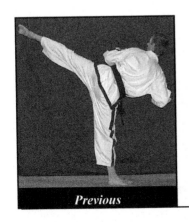    

Previous   *Moves 45c & 46*

Sonkal Najunde Daebi Makgi
Low Knifehand Guarding Block

Yop Cha Momchau
Side Checking Kick

47. Bring your Left foot forwards and out to your Left, pivoting 30 degrees anti-clockwise to form a *Right L-Stance* while executing a *Low Knifehand Guarding Block.*

48a. Maintain your direction and execute a *Side Checking Kick* with your Right leg.

Previous   *Moves 47 & 48a*

Nopunde Yop Cha Tulgi
High Side Thrusting Kick

Nopunde Bandae Dollyo Chagi
High Reverse Turning Kick

Note: Movements 48a & 48b are performed as *'Consecutive Kicks'*

48b. Without placing your Right foot down, re-chamber and execute a *High Side Thrusting Kick* with your Right leg.

49a. Maintain your direction and place your Right foot down in front, then execute a *High Reverse Turning Kick* with your Left leg.

Previous   *Moves 48b & 49a*

Nopunde Dollyo Chagi
High Turning Kick

Note: Movements 49a & 49b are performed as *'Consecutive Kicks'*

Gokgaeng-i Chagi
Pick-Shape Kick

49b. Without placing your Left foot down, re-chamber and execute a *High Turning Kick* with your Left leg.

50. Maintain your direction and place your Left foot down in front, then execute a *Pick-Shape Kick* with your Right leg.

Previous   *Moves 49b & 50*

**Nopunde Bandalson
Bandae Bandal Taeragi**
*High Arc-Hand Reverse
Crescent Strike*

Dwit Palkup Tulgi
Back Elbow Thrust

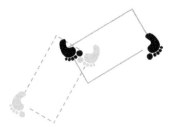

51. Following the previous kick, bring your Right foot down in front to form a *Right Walking Stance* while executing a *High Arc-Hand Reverse Crescent Strike* with your Left hand.

52. Bring your Right foot back to your Left foot, then move your Left foot out to the side while pivoting your body 60 degrees anti-clockwise to form a *Left Diagonal Stance*. Simultaneously execute a *Back Elbow Thrust* with your Right elbow, placing your Left hand on your Right fist.

Previous   *Moves 51 & 52*

**Sondung Nopunde Bakuro
Taeragi**
Back-Hand High Outward Strike

Nopunde Anuro Bandal Chagi
High Inside Crescent Kick

53. In the direction you are now facing, move your Left foot forwards in a *stamping* motion to form a *Right L-Stance* while executing a *Back-Hand Outward Strike* with your Left hand.

54a. Maintaining the 30 angle you are currently travelling and execute a *High Inside Crescent Kick* to your Left Palm with your Right leg.

Previous

Moves 53 & 54a

 # 54b

 # 55a

Nopunde Yop Cha Jirugi
High Side Piercing Kick

Note: Movements 54a & 54b are performed as *'Consecutive Kicks'*

Sondung Nopunde Bakuro Taeragi
Back-Hand High Outward Strike

54b. Following the previous kick and without placing your foot down, re-chamber and execute a *High Side Piercing Kick* with your Right leg.

55a. Following the previous kick, lower your Right foot in front to form a *Left L-Stance* while executing a *Back-Hand Outward Strike* with your Right hand.

Previous

Moves 54b & 55a

**Kaunde Baro Ap
Joomok Jirugi**
*Middle Obverse
Forefist Punch*

Orun Gutja Makgi
Right 9-Shape Block

Wen Gutja Makgi
Left 9-Shape Block

> **Note:**
> Movements 56a
> & 56b are
> performed in
> *'Continuous
> Motion'*

55b. Maintain your stance and execute a *Left Obverse Forefist Punch* to your Right palm.

56a. Maintain the direction and angle you are travelling in, pivot on your Right foot, moving your Left foot anti-clockwise (forwards) to form a *Sitting Stance* while executing a *Right 9-Shape Block*.

56b. Maintain your stance and execute a *Left 9-Shape Block*.

Previous   *Moves 55b, 56a & 56b*

Yop Joomok Naerjo Taeragi
Side Fist Downward Strike

Digutja Jirugi
U-Shape Punch

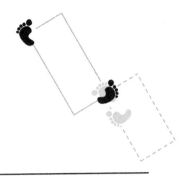

57. Moving back in the opposite direction, bring your Left foot towards your Right foot to form a *Left Vertical Stance* while executing a *Side Fist Downward Strike* with your Right hand.

58. Maintain your current direction and move your Left foot forwards to form a *Left Fixed Stance* while executing a *U-Shape Punch*.

Previous　　　　　*Moves 57 & 58*

Twimyo Dwit Cha Jirugi
Flying Back Piercing Kick

Sonkal Yop Taeragi
Knifehand Side Strike

59a. Jump up and execute a *Flying Back Piercing Kick* with your Right Leg (in the current direction). **GTF Note:** In the GTF this is sometimes termed a *Jumping Turning Side Piercing Kick*.

59b. Following the previous flying kick, land to form a *Left L-Stance* while executing a *Knifehand Side Strike* with your Right hand.

Previous   *Moves 59a & 59b*

Dwit Cha Jirugi
Back Piercing Kick

Nopunde Bandal Jirugi
High Crescent Punch

60a. While maintaining your current direction, execute a *Back Piercing Kick* with your Left leg.

60b. Following the previous kick, lower your foot to form a *Left Walking Stance* while executing a *High Crescent Punch* with your Right hand.

Previous

Moves 60a & 60b

**Najunde Sonkal
Yop Makgi**
Low Knifehand Side Block

Sonbadak Duro Makgi
Palm Scooping Block

**Kaunde Ap Joomok
Jirugi**
Middle Forefist Punch

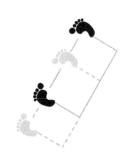

61. Move your Right foot forwards, then outwards to your Right to form a *Sitting Stance* facing approximately North-West at 30 degrees and execute a *Low Knifehand Side Block* with your Left hand.

62a. Maintaining your stance and angle, slide to your Right while executing a Palm Scooping Block with your Right hand.

62b. Maintain your stance and execute a *Middle Forefist Punch* with your Left fist.

Previous

Moves 61, 62a & 62b

**Durokamyo
Yop Cha Milgi**
Skipping Side Pushing Kick

Nopunde Bandae Dollyo Chagi
High Reverse Turning Kick

**Nopunde Sonkal
Yop Makgi**
*High Knifehand
Side Block*

63a. Skip to your Right by moving your Left foot in place of your Right foot and execute a *Side Pushing Kick* with your Right leg.

63b. Maintaining your current direction, following the previous kick, lower your Right foot to your side and execute a *High Reverse Turning Kick* with your Left leg.

63c. Following the previous kick, lower your Left foot in front to form a *Left Walking Stance* while executing a *High Knifehand Side Block* with your Left hand.

Previous   *Moves 63a, 63b & 63c*

Mikulmyo Ap Cha Milgi
Sliding Front Pushing Kick

Nopunde Opun Sonkut Tulgi
High Flat Fingertip Thrust

64a. Maintain your current direction and execute a *Sliding Front Pushing Kick* with your Right leg.

64b. Following the previous kick, lower your Right foot in front to form a *Right Walking Stance* while executing a *High Flat Fingertip Thrust* with your Right hand.

Previous   *Moves 64a & 64b*

**Yop Joomok Kaunde
Yop Taeragi**
Side-Fist Middle Side Strike

Sonbadak Duro Makgi
Palm Scooping Block

Ap Joomok Jirugi
Forefist Punch

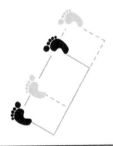

65. Move your Right foot to your centre-line and pivot 180 degrees, move your Left foot forwards in a *stamping* motion to form a *Sitting Stance* while executing a *Side-Fist Middle Side Strike* with your Left fist.

66a. While maintaining your stance and angle, slide to your Left while executing a *Palm Scooping Block* with your Left hand.

66b. Maintain your stance and execute a *Middle Forefist Punch* with your Right fist.

Previous   *Moves 65, 66a & 66b*

66c

67a

Najunde Sonkal Yop Makgi
Low Knifehand Side Block

Durokamyo Yop Cha Milgi
Skipping Side Pushing Kick

66c. Maintain your stance and execute a *Low Knifehand Side Block* with your Right hand, turning your head to face to your Right.

67a. Skip to your Left by moving your Right foot in place of your Left foot and executing a *Side Pushing Kick* with your Left leg.

Previous   *Moves 66c & 67a*

Nopunde Bandae Dollyo Chagi
High Reverse Turning Kick

Nopunde Sonkal Yop Makgi
High Kinifehand Side Block

67b. Maintaining your current direction, and following the previous kick, lower your Left foot to your side and execute a *High Reverse Turning Kick* with your Right leg.

67c. Following the previous kick, lower your Right foot in front to form a *Right Walking Stance* while executing a *High Knifehand Side Block* with your Right hand.

Previous   *Moves 67b & 67c*

Nopunde Dollyo Chagi
High Turning Kick

Ban Gunnon Sogi,
Ap Joomok Naeryo Jirugi
Half Walking Stance,
Forefist Downward Punch

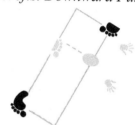

68a. Drop to the floor by bending your Left knee and placing your hands to your side and execute a *High Turning Kick* in the direction your were travelling (at a 30 degree angle).

68b. Following the previous kick, lower your Left foot in front to form a *Right Half Walking Stance* while executing a *Downward Punch* with your Left fist.

Previous   *Moves 68a & 68b*

Yang Ban Da Ri
Sitting Cross Legged
(Fists On Top Of Knees)

Return. Upon completion of the pattern, bring your right foot backwards and behind your Left leg, sitting back into the ready position of *Sitting Cross Legged with fists on top of knees.*

Previous — *Return to Ready Posture*

Tips For Sun-Duk Hyung

1. This patterns has a lot of techniques executed at 30 degree angles, however, it is the change of positioning between these angles and travelling straight (forwards, backwards or sideward's) that can be confusing, so it is useful to note some reference points around the area you are performing to keep all the angles/positions in the same direction - at least until you know the pattern inside out!

2. The Palm Pressing Blocks (moves #24 and #25) are performed the same way as in Choi-Yong, in a '*walking*' type motion, as opposed to pausing slightly between them.

So-San
Great Monk Choi Hyong Ung

서 산 틀

So-San is the pseudonym of the great monk Choi Hyong Ung (1520-1604) during the Lee Dynasty. So-San has 72 movements which refer to his age when he organized a corps of monk soldiers with the assistance of his pupil Sa Myunh Dang. The monk soldiers helped repulse the Japanese pirates who overran most of the Korean peninsula in 1592.

Ready Posture

1

2

Moa Junbi Sogi 'A'
Closed Ready Stance 'A'

Kaunde Palmok Daebi Makgi
Middle Forearm Guarding Block

Kaunde Sewo Jirugi
Middle Vertical Punch

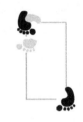

1. From *Closed Ready Stance 'A'*, slide your Right leg backwards approximately one stance length to form a *Right Rear Foot Stance* while executing a *Middle Forearm Guarding Block*.

2. Without stepping forwards, shift your Left foot to form a *Left Walking Stance* and execute a *Middle Vertical Punch* with your Right fist.

The slide when performing the 1st movement

From the ready posture to moves 1 & 2

204

Kaunde Palmok Daebi Makgi
Middle Forearm Guarding Block

Kaunde Sewo Jirugi
Middle Vertical Punch

Nopunde Sonkal Yop Makgi
High Knifehand Side Block

3. *Slide* your Left leg backwards approximately one stance length to form a *Left Rear Foot Stance* while executing a *Middle Forearm Guarding Block*.

4. Without stepping forwards, shift your Right foot to form a *Right Walking Stance* and execute a *Middle Vertical Punch* with your Left fist.

5. Pivot 135 degrees anti-clockwise into a *Left Walking Stance* and execute a *High Knifehand Side Block* with your Right hand.

Previous　　　　　　　　　　　　　　　　*Moves 3, 4 & 5*

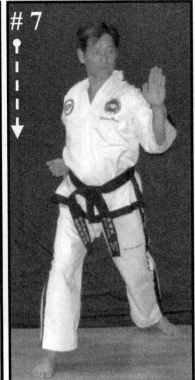

**Kaunde Ap
Joomok Jirugi**
Middle Forefist Punch

Nopunde Sonkal Yop Makgi
High Knifehand Side Block

**Kaunde Ap
Joomok Jirugi**
Middle Forefist Punch

ITF Note: Movements 5 & 6 are performed in *'Fast Motion'*

ITF Note: Movements 7 & 8 are performed in *'Fast Motion'*

6. Pivot 90 degrees clockwise (so you remain at a 45 degree angle) into a *Sitting Stance* and execute a *Middle Forefist Punch* with your Left fist.

7. Pivot 90 degrees clockwise (so you are facing forwards again) into a *Right Walking Stance* and execute a *High Knifehand Side Block* with your Left hand.

8. Pivot 90 degrees anti-clockwise into a *Sitting Stance* (returning to the same position as #6 at a 45 degree angle) and execute a *Middle Forefist Punch* with your Right fist.

Previous

Moves 6, 7 & 8

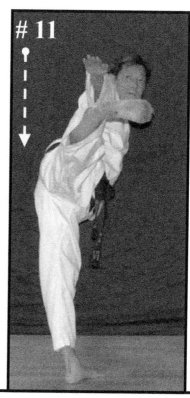

**Sang Sonkal
Soopyong Taeragi**
*Twin Knifehand
Horizontal Strike*

Nopunde Yop Cha Jirugi
High Side Piercing Kick

Nopunde Dollyo Chagi
High Turning Kick

Note: Movements 10 & 11 are performed as *'Consecutive Kicks'*

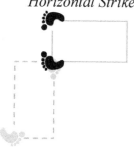

9. Moving your Right foot, pivot 135 degrees clockwise to form a *Parallel Stance* and execute a *Twin Knifehand Horizontal Strike*.

10. Raise your Right leg and execute a *High Side Piercing Kick* to your Right hand side. Maintain the position of your arms as they were in move 9.

11. Without lowering your Right leg, pivot 180 degrees anti-clockwise and execute a *High Turning Kick*. Maintain the position of your arms as they were in moves 9 an 10.

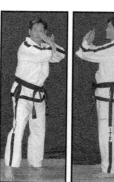
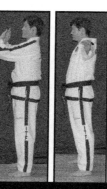
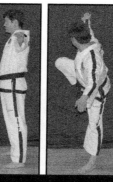

Previous   *Moves 9, 10 & 11*

**Nopunde Dung Joomok
Yop Taeragi**
High Back Fist Side Strike

**Sang Sonkal
Soopyong Taeragi**
*Twin Knifehand
Horizontal Strike*

Nopunde Yop Cha Jirugi
High Side Piercing Kick

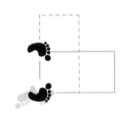

12. Following the previous kick, lower your Right foot and jump into a *Right X-Stance* angled at 45 degrees and execute *High Back Fist Side Strike* with your Right fist, bringing your Left finger belly to the side of your fist.

13. Move your Left foot to form a *Parallel Stance* and execute a *Twin Knifehand Horizontal Strike*.

14. Raise your Left leg and execute a *High Side Piercing Kick* to your Left hand side. Maintain the position of your arms as they were in move 13.

Previous   *Moves 12, 13 & 14*

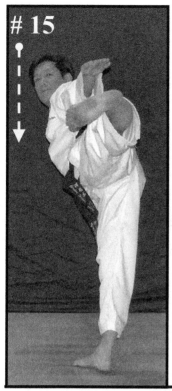

Nopunde Dollyo Chagi
High Turning Kick

Nopunde Dung Joomok Yop Taeragi
High Back Fist Side Strike

Najunde Doo Joomok Jirugi
Low Double Fist Punch

Note: Movements 14 & 15 are performed as *'Consecutive Kicks'*

15. Without lowering your Left leg, pivot 180 degrees clockwise and execute a *High Turning Kick*. Maintain the position of your arms as they were in moves 13 and 14.

16. Following the previous kick, lower your Left foot and jump into a *Left X-Stance* angled at 45 degrees and execute a *High Back Fist Side Strike* with your Left fist, bringing your Right finger belly to the side of your fist.

17. Move your Left foot outwards (90 degrees relative to your current position) to form a *Right L-Stance* and execute a *Low Double Fist Punch*.

Previous — *Moves 15, 16 & 17*

Jappyolsol Tae
Release Move

**Nopunde Bandae
Ap Joomok Jirugi**
High Reverse Forefist Punch

---

18. Bring your Right palm to the underside of your Left fist then twist both hands anti-clockwise, while simultaneously slipping your Left foot into a *Left Walking Stance* to perform a *Release Move*.

19. Maintain your stance and execute a *High Reverse Forefist Punch* with your Right fist.

Previous   *Moves 18 & 19*

Najunde Doo Joomok Jirugi
Low Double Fist Punch

Jappyolsol Tae
Release Move

20. Perform a centre-line turn into a *Left L-Stance* and execute a *Low Double Fist Punch*.

21. Bring your Left palm to the underside of your Right fist then twist both hands clockwise, while simultaneously slipping your Right foot into a *Right Walking Stance* to perform a *Release Move*.

Previous

Moves 20 & 21

Reversed view of #20

22

23

**Nopunde Bandae
Ap Joomok Jirugi**
High Reverse Forefist Punch

**Joongi Joomok Kaunde
Dwijibun Jirugi**
Middle Knuckle Fist Upset Punch

---

22. Maintain your stance and execute a *High Reverse Forefist Punch* with your Left fist.

23. *Slide* forwards to form a *Right L-Stance* while executing a *Right Middle Knuckle Fist Upset Punch*, bringing your Left fist in to your Right shoulder.

Previous

Moves 22 & 23

Dung Joomok Bandae Ap Taeragi
Backfist Reverse Front Strike

**Joongi Joomok Kaunde
Dwijibun Jirugi**
Middle Knuckle Fist Upset Punch

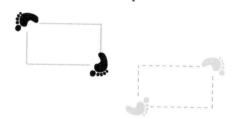

24. Slip into a *Left Walking Stance* by moving your rear foot and execute a *Front Back Fist Strike* with your Right fist, bringing your Left fist under your elbow.

25. Pivoting on your Left foot, turn 180 degrees clockwise and *slide* into a *Left L-Stance* while executing a *Left Middle Knuckle Fist Upset Punch*, bringing your Right fist into your Left shoulder.

Previous

Moves 24 & 25

Dung Joomok Bandae Ap Taeragi
Backfist Reverse Front Strike

Gunnon Junbi Sogi
Walking Ready Stance

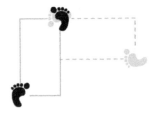

26. Slip into a *Right Walking Stance* by moving your rear foot and execute a *Front Back Fist Strike* with your Left fist, bringing your Right fist under your elbow.

27. Move your Left (back) foot 90 degrees clockwise to form a *Right Walking Ready Stance*.

Previous   *Moves 26 & 27*

Twimyo Ap Cha Jirugi
Flying Front Snap Kick

**Kaunde Sonkal
Daebi Makgi**
*Middle Knifehand
Guarding Block*

**Bakat Palmok
Nopunde Ap Makgi**
*Outer Forearm
High Front Block*

28. Jump and execute a *Flying Front Snap Kick* with your Right leg. Perform in '*double motion*' (AKA 'bicycle motion')

29. Land from the previous kick in a *Left L-Stance* and execute a *Middle Knifehand Guarding Block*.

30. Move your Right foot back to form a *Left Walking Stance* while executing an *Outer Forearm High Front Block* with your Right arm.

Previous

Moves 28, 29 & 30

Kaunde Ap
Joomok Jirugi
Middle Forefist Punch

Bakat Palmok
Nopunde Ap Makgi
Outer Forearm
High Front Block

Kaunde Ap
Joomok Jirugi
Middle Forefist Punch

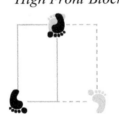

31. *Shift* forwards (approximately half a stance), but maintain your stance and execute a *Left Middle Forefist Punch.*

32. Pivot 180 degrees on your Left foot moving your Right foot to form a *Right Walking Stance.* Execute an *Outer Forearm High Front Block* with your Left arm.

33. *Shift* forwards (approximately half a stance), but maintain your stance and execute a *Right Middle Forefist Punch.*

Previous

Moves 35, 36 & 37

Sliding from #30 to #31

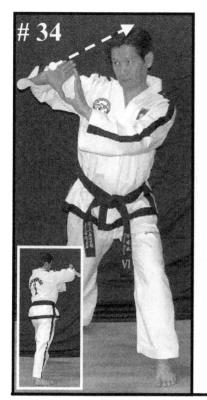

Doo Bandalson Kaunde Makgi
Double Arc-Hand Middle Block

Anuro Sonkal Taeragi
Inward Knifehand Strike

An Palmok Dollimyo Makgi
Inner Forearm Circular Block

34. Without moving forwards, pivot your feet 135 degrees anti-clockwise to form a *Left Walking Stance* and execute a *Double Arc Hand Middle Block*.

35. Maintain your stance and execute a *High Inward Knifehand Strike* with your Right hand, bringing Left fist to Right shoulder.

36. Without stepping, pivot your feet 135 degrees clockwise to form a *Right Walking Stance* and execute a *Left Inner Forearm Circular Block* at a 45 degree angle.

Previous — Moves 34, 35 & 36

**Nopunde Ap
Joomok Jirugi**
High Forefist Punch

**Najunde Ap Cha
Busigi**
Low Front Snap Kick

**Kaunde Ap Joomok
Jirugi**
Middle Forefist Punch

37. Maintain your stance and execute a *High Forefist Punch* with your Right hand.

38. Execute a *Low Front Snap Kick* with your Left leg. Maintain the position of your arms as they were in move 37.

39. Following the kick, land in a *Left Walking Stance* while executing a *Middle Forefist Punch* with your Left hand.

Previous

Moves 37, 38 & 39

Kaunde Bandae Ap Joomok Jirugi	**Kyocha Sonkal Chookyo Makgi**	**Doo Bandalson Kaunde Makgi**
Middle Reverse Forefist Punch	*X-Knifehand Rising Block*	*Double Arc-Hand Middle Block*

ITF Note: Movements 39 & 40 are performed in *'Fast Motion'*

40. Maintain your stance and execute a *Middle Reverse Forefist Punch* with your Right hand.

41. Maintain your stance and execute a *X-Knifehand Rising Block*.

42. Without stepping, pivot 135 degrees clockwise to form a *Right Walking Stance* and execute a *Double Arc-Hand Middle Block*.

   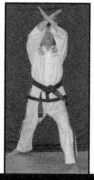  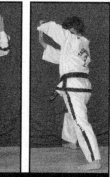

Previous — *Moves 40, 41 & 42*

Anuro Sonkal Taeragi
Inward Knifehand Strike

An Palmok
Dollimyo Makgi
Inner Forearm Circular Block

Nopunde Ap
Joomok Jirugi
High Forefist Punch

43. Maintain your stance and execute a *High Inward Knifehand Strike* with your Left hand, bringing your Right fist to your Left shoulder.

44. Without stepping, pivot your feet 135 degrees anti-clockwise to form a *Left Walking Stance* and execute a *Right Inner Forearm Circular Block* at a 45 degree angle.

45. Maintain your stance and execute a *High Forefist Punch* with your Left hand.

Previous   *Moves 43, 44 & 45*

**Najunde Ap
Cha Busigi**
Low Front Snap Kick

**Kaunde Ap
Joomok Jirugi**
Middle Forefist Punch

**Kaunde Bandae Ap
Joomok Jirugi**
*Middle Reverse Forefist
Punch*

ITF Note: Movements 47 & 48 are performed in *'Fast Motion'*

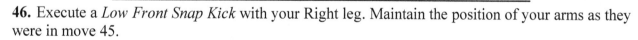

46. Execute a *Low Front Snap Kick* with your Right leg. Maintain the position of your arms as they were in move 45.

47. Following the kick, land in a *Right Walking Stance* while executing a *Middle Forefist Punch* with your Right hand.

48. Maintain your stance and execute a *Middle Reverse Forefist Punch* with your Left hand.

Previous　　　*Moves 46, 47 & 48*

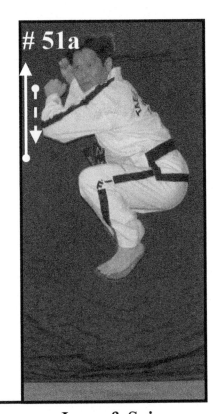

**Kyocha Sonkal
Chookyo Makgi**
X-Knifehand Rising Block

**Najunde Sonkal
Daebi Makgi**
*Low Knifehand
Guarding Block*

Jump & Spin
180 Degrees Anti-Clockwise

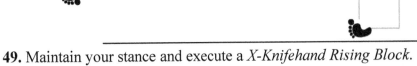

49. Maintain your stance and execute a *X-Knifehand Rising Block*.

50. Move your Left foot forwards just past your Right foot, then pivot (on your Left foot), turning 180 degrees anti-clockwise and slide back to form a *Right L-Stance* while executing a *Low Knifehand Guarding Block*.

51a. Jump forwards, spinning 180 degrees anti-clockwise as you do so.

Previous　　　　　　　　　　　*Moves 49, 50 & 51a*

51b

52

53

Kaunde Palmok Daebi Makgi
Middle Forearm Guarding Block

Kaunde An Palmok Makgi / Najunde Sonkal Makgi
Middle Inner Forearm Block / Low Knifehand Block

Nopunde Bandae Ap Joomok Jirugi
High Reverse Forefist Punch

ITF Note: Movements 52 & 53 are performed in *'Continuous Motion'*

51b. Following the jump, land in a *Right L-Stance* simultaneously executing a *Middle Forearm Guarding Block*.

52. Slip your Left foot to form a *Left Walking Stance* and simultaneously execute a *Middle Inner Forearm Block* with your Left arm and a *Low Knifehand Block* with your Right arm.

53. Maintain your stance and execute a *High Reverse Forefist Punch* with your Right arm.

Previous

Moves 51b, 52 & 53

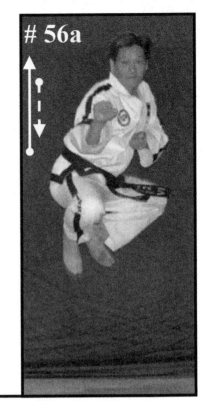

Kaunde Ap
Joomok Jirugi
Middle Forefist Punch

Najunde Sonkal
Daebi Makgi
Low Knifehand
Guarding Block

Jump & Spin
180 Degrees
Anti-Clockwise

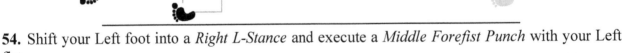

54. Shift your Left foot into a *Right L-Stance* and execute a *Middle Forefist Punch* with your Left fist.

55. Move your Right foot forwards just past your Left foot, then pivot (on your Right foot), turning 180 degree's clockwise and slide back to form a *Left L-Stance* while executing a *Low Knifehand Guarding Block*.

56a. Jump forwards, spinning 180 degrees clockwise as you do so.

Previous   *Moves 54, 55 & 56a*

 # 56b

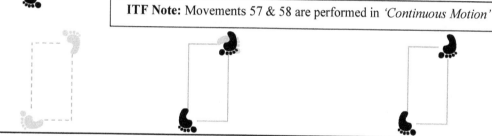

 # 57

 # 58

**Kaunde Palmok
Daebi Makgi**
*Middle Forearm
Guarding Block*

**Kaunde An Palmok Makgi /
Najunde Sonkal Makgi**
*Middle Inner Forearm Block /
Low Knifehand Block*

**Nopunde Bandae Ap
Joomok Jirugi**
High Reverse Forefist Punch

ITF Note: Movements 57 & 58 are performed in *'Continuous Motion'*

56b. Following the jump, land in a *Left L-Stance* simultaneously executing a *Middle Forearm Guarding Block*.

57. Slip your Right foot to form a *Right Walking Stance* and simultaneously execute a *Middle Inner Forearm Block* with your Right arm and a *Low Knifehand Block* with your Left arm.

58. Maintain your stance and execute a *High Reverse Forefist Punch* with your Left arm.

Previous *Moves 56b, 57 & 58*

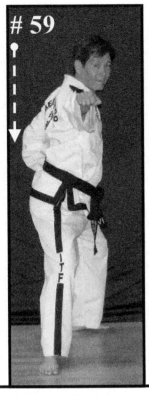

**Kaunde Ap
Joomok Jirugi**
Middle Forefist Punch

**Sonbadak
Duro Makgi**
Palm Scooping Block

Kaunde Ap Joomok Jirugi
Middle Forefist Punch

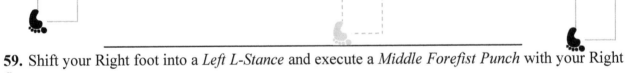

59. Shift your Right foot into a *Left L-Stance* and execute a *Middle Forefist Punch* with your Right fist.

60. Move your Right foot back, just beyond your Left Foot then *slide* backwards into a *Left L-Stance* and execute a *Palm Scooping Block* with your Right hand.

61. Maintaining your *Left L-Stance*, *shift* forwards approximately half a stance length and execute a *Middle Forefist Punch* with your Left fist.

Previous

Moves 59, 60 & 61

Goburyo Junbi Sogi 'A'
Bending Ready Stance 'A'

Nopunde Yop Cha Jirugi
High Side Piercing Kick

**Kaunde Bandae
Ap Joomok Jirugi**
*Middle Reverse
Forefist Punch*

62. Taking your weight on your Left foot, rotate 180 degrees clockwise and form a *Bending Ready Stance 'A'*.

63. Execute a *High Side Piercing Kick* with your Right leg.

64. Following the kick, lower your leg to form a *Right Walking Stance* and execute a *Reverse Forefist Punch* with your Left fist.

Previous   *Moves 62, 63 & 64*

**Kaunde Sonkal
Daebi Makgi**
*Middle Knifehand
Guarding Block*

**Sonbadak
Duro Makgi**
Palm Scooping Block

**Kaunde Ap
Joomok Jirugi**
Middle Forefist Punch

65. Move your Right foot backwards to form a *Right L-Stance* and execute a *Middle Knifehand Guarding Block*.

66. Move your Left foot back, just beyond your Right Foot then slide backwards into a *Right L-Stance* and execute a *Palm Scooping Block* with your Left hand.

67. Maintaining your *Right L-Stance*, shift forwards approximately half a stance length and execute a *Middle Forefist Punch* with your Right fist.

Previous   *Moves 65, 66 & 67*

Goburyo Junbi Sogi 'A'
Bending Ready Stance 'A'

Nopunde Yop Cha Jirugi
High Side Piercing Kick

**Kaunde Bandae
Ap Joomok Jirugi**
*Middle Reverse
Forefist Punch*

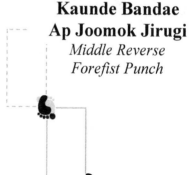

68. Taking your weight on your Right foot, rotate 180 degrees anti-clockwise and form a *Bending Ready Stance 'A'*.

69. Execute a *High Side Piercing Kick* with your Left leg.

70. Following the kick, lower your leg to form a *Left Walking Stance* and execute a *Reverse Forefist Punch* with your Right fist.

Previous   *Moves 49 & 50*

**Kaunde Sonkal
Daebi Makgi**
*Middle Knifehand
Guarding Block*

**Nopunde Ap
Joomok Jirugi**
High Forefist Punch

Moa Junbi Sogi 'A'
Closed Ready Stance 'A'

ITF Note: Movements 71 & 72 are performed in *'Continuous Motion'*

71. Move your Left foot backwards to form a *Left L-Stance* and execute a *Middle Knifehand Guarding Block*.

72. Shift your front foot into a *Right Walking Stance* and execute a *High Forefist Punch* with your Right fist.

Return. Upon completion of the pattern, bring your Right foot backwards to *Closed Ready Stance 'A'*.

Previous   *Moves 71, 72 & return to Ready Stance*

Tips For So-San Tul

1. To perform this pattern properly make sure the first movement has the same power as the last.

2. So-San is a long pattern so either pace yourself, get fitter or do both.

3. This is a great pattern to *wow* students when they see you perform 72 movements and get back to the start position, hence lots of practice is required, more so to gauge the shifts and jumps in this pattern.

Se-Jong
Greatest Korean King

세

종

틀

Se-Jong is named after the greatest Korean King, Se-Jong, who invented the Korean alphabet in 1443, and was also a noted meteorologist. Se-Jong has 24 movements which refer to the 24 letters of the Korean alphabet, while the diagram represents the King.

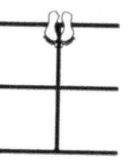

Ready Posture

1

2

Moa Junbi Sogi 'B'
Closed Ready Stance 'B'

Najunde Bakat Palmok Makgi
Low Outer Forearm Block

Sang Palmok Makgi
Twin Forearm Block

1. From the ready posture (*Moa Junbi Sogi 'B'*), move your Left foot to your Left to form a *Left Walking Stance* while executing a *Low Outer Forearm Block* with your Left arm.

2. Move foot to foot by bringing your Left foot to your Right foot, pivot 180 degrees and step out with your Right foot to form a *Left L-Stance* while executing a *Twin Forearm Block*.

From the ready posture to moves 1 & 2

Kaunde Yop Cha Jirugi
Middle Side Piercing Kick

Bakat Palmok Chookyo Makgi
Outer Forearm Rising Block

3. Taking your weight on your Left foot, execute a *Right Middle Side Piercing Kick*, 90 degrees anti-clockwise from your previous position.

4. Lower your Right foot (approximately 1 shoulder width from your left foot), then pivot 90 degrees anti-clockwise and move your Left foot forwards to form a *Left Walking Stance* while executing a *Left Outer Forearm Rising Block*.

Previous | *Moves 3 & 4*

Kaunde Sonkal Taeragi
Middle Knifehand Strike

Moa Junbi Sogi 'B'
Closed Ready Stance 'B'

5. Move foot to foot by bringing your Left foot to your Right foot, then move your Right foot outwards to form a *Sitting Stance* while executing a *Middle Knifehand Strike* with your Right hand.

6. Move your Right foot back in towards your Left foot to form a *Closed Ready Stance 'B'*.

Previous

Moves 5 & 6

**Dung Joomok
Yop Taeragi**
Back Fist Side Strike

Nopunde Ap Joomok Jirugi
High Forefist Punch

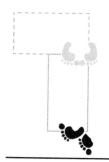

7. Jump forwards into a *Left X-Stance* and execute a *High Back Fist Side Strike* with your Left fist, bringing your Right finger belly to the side of your fist.

8. Pivot 90 degrees clockwise and move your Right foot to form a Right Walking Stance while executing a *High Forefist Punch* with your Right hand.

Previous

Moves 7 & 8

**Nopunde Palmok
Daebi Makgi**
High Forearm Guarding Block

Sun Sonkut Tulgi
Straight Fingertip Thrust

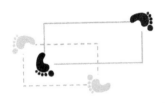

9. Perform a centre line turn to form a *Left Fixed Stance* while executing a *High Forearm Guarding Block*.

10. Move your Right foot forwards to form a *Right Walking Stance* while executing a *Straight Fingertip Thrust* with your Right hand.

Previous

Moves 9 & 10

**Dung Joomok Nopunde
Yop Taeragi**
High Backfist Side Strike

Sonbadak Duro Makgi
Palm Scooping Block

11. Move foot to foot by bringing your Right foot to your Left. Pivoting 180 degrees anti-clockwise, move your Left foot forwards to form a *Left Walking Stance* while executing a *High Backfist Side Strike* with your left fist.

12. Move your Left foot inline with your Right foot to form a *Sitting Stance* at 90 degrees clockwise from your previous position and execute a *Palm Scooping Block* with your Left hand.

Previous

Moves 12 & 13

Kaunde Dollyo Chagi
Middle Turning Kick

Nopunde Doo Palmok Makgi
High Double Forearm Block

Extend Right Fist Horizontally
(slow motion)

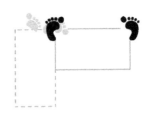

13. Execute a *Middle Turning Kick* with your Left leg in the direction you are facing.

14. Lower your Left foot but do not place it on the ground. Instead, jump forwards (approximately one stance length, in the direction of the kick), landing in a *Left X-Stance* while executing a *High Double Forearm Block*.

15. Move your Right foot outwards to form a *Sitting Stance* and extend your Right Fist. Perform in slow motion.

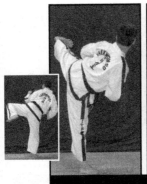

Previous

Moves 13, 14 & 15

Dung Joomok
Ap Taeragi
Backfist Front Strike

Step Left
Right Foot Behind
Left Foot

Sang Sonbadak
Noollo Makgi
Twin Palm Pressing Block

16. Maintain your stance and execute a *Backfist Front Strike* with your Left fist, bringing your Right first underneath your elbow.

17a. Move to your left by moving your Right foot directly behind your Left foot, chambering the next block as you do so.

17b. Continue by moving your Left foot to form a *Left Diagonal Stance* and execute a *Twin Palm Pressing Block*.

Previous

Moves 16, 17a & 17b

Doo Bandalson Kaunde Makgi
Double Arc-Hand Middle Block

Nopunde Bakat Palmok Yop Makgi / Najunde Bakat Palmok Yop Makgi
High Outer Forearm Side Block / Low Outer Forearm Side Block

18. Pivot your feet to form a *Left Walking Stance* and execute a *Double Arc-Hand Middle Block*.

19. Taking your weight on your Right leg, pull your Left foot (Reverse Footsword) to the side of your Right knee to form a Right One-Leg Stance, simultaneously executing a *Right High Outer Forearm Side Block* and a *Left Low Outer Forearm Side Block*.

Previous

Moves 18 & 19

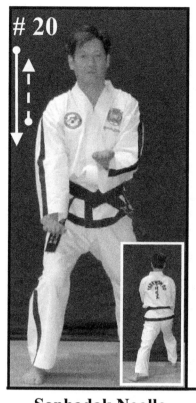

Sonbadak Noollo Makgi
Palm Pressing Block (slow motion)

Dung Joomok Yop Ap Taergai
Back Fist Front Strike

Yop Palkup Tulgi
Side Elbow Thrust

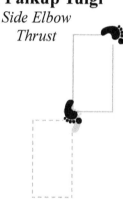

20. Lower your Left foot to the rear to form a *Right Walking Stance* while executing a *Right Palm Pressing Block.* Perform in slow motion.

21. Taking your weight on your Right leg, pull your Left instep to the rear of your Right knee to form a *Right One-Leg Stance* while executing a *High Back Fist Front Strike* with your Right fist, striking your Left palm with the back forearm as you do so.

22. Lower your Left foot while pivoting 180 degrees clockwise and drop into a *Right Fixed Stance* while executing a *Side Elbow Thrust* with your Left elbow.

Previous   *Moves 20, 21 & 22*

Nopunde Sonkal Daebi Makgi
High Knifehand Guarding Block

Kaunde Ap Joomok Jirugi
Middle Forefist Punch

Moa Junbi Sogi 'B'
Closed Ready Stance 'B'

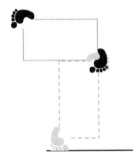  

23. Pivoting on your Left foot, move your Right foot 90 degrees clockwise to form a *Left L-Stance* and execute a *High Knifehand Guarding Block*.

24. Step foot to foot by bringing your Right foot to your Left foot. Pivoting 180 degrees, move your Left foot forwards to form a *Right L-Stance* while executing a *Right Middle Forefist Punch*.

Return. Move your left foot back into *Moa Junbi Sogi 'B'*.

Previous   *Moves 23, 24 & return to Ready Posture*

Tips For Se-Jong Tul

1. Although this pattern is only 24 movements, it is performed at 5th Dan level within the ITF (expert status) so every single move should be as it should be i.e.. Exact and perfect. Unlike a lot of patterns there is no mirroring of movements as each move is different.

2. For move #4, remember to bring the left foot forward otherwise you will miss the return mark.

3. Move #20 is a Walking Stance and not performed in a Low Stance as you usually find with Pressing Blocks within the patterns.

Tong-Il
Reunification

통

일

틀

Tong-Il denotes the resolution of the unification of Korea which has been divided since 1945. The diagram symbolizes the homogenous race. Move 1 of Tong-Il represents a united Korea, the homeland of General Choi, move 2 represents a country divided and move 38 represents breaking through the 38th parallel. The various stamping motions represent the Generals frustration of his motherland divided.

**Sonkal Moa
Narani Sogi***
*Parallel Stance with
Overlapped Back-hand*

**Sang Joomok
Kaunde Ap Jirugi**
*Twin Fist Middle
Front Punch
(slow motion)*

1. From the ready posture (*Parallel Stance with Overlapped Back-hand*) move your Right leg backwards to form a *Left Walking Stance* while executing a *Twin Fist Middle Punch*. Perform in slow motion.

* There is no 'official' terminology for this ready posture, except the English version, however the hands form two knifehands and they are close or overlapped and the Korean word for 'close' is 'Moa'.

From the ready posture to move 1

Sang Sonkal Soopyong Taeragi
Twin Knifehand Horizontal Strike
(slow motion)

Bakat Palmok Kaunde
Anuro Makgi
Outer Forearm Middle
Inward Block

2. Move your Left leg backwards to form a *Right Walking Stance* while executing a *Twin Knifehand Horizontal Strike.* Perform in slow motion.

3. Move your Left foot forwards to form a *Right Rear Foot Stance* while executing an *Outer Forearm Middle Inward Block* with your Left arm.

Previous   *Moves 2 & 3*

**Sonbadak Najunde
Anuro Makgi**
Palm Low Inward Block

**Kaunde Bandae
Ap Joomok Jirugi**
*Middle Reverse
Forefist Punch*

**Kaunde Ap
Joomok Jirugi**
Middle Forefist Punch

ITF Note: Movements 5 & 6 are performed in *'Fast Motion'*

4. Move your Right leg back to form a *Left Walking Stance* while executing a *Palm Low Inward Block* with your Right palm while bringing your Left fist to your Right shoulder.

5. Move your Right foot forwards to form a *Left L-Stance* while executing a *Middle Reverse Forefist Punch* with your Right fist.

6. Maintain your previous stance and execute a *Middle Forefist Punch* with your Left fist.

Previous   *Moves 4, 5 & 6*

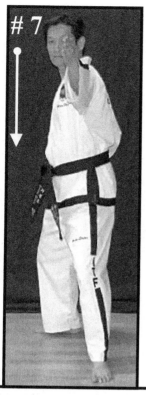

**Sondung Nopunde
Bakuro Taeragi**
*Back-Hand High
Outward Strike*

**Nopunde Anuro
Sewo Chagi**
High Inward Vertical Kick

**Sondung Nopunde
Bakuro Taeragi**
*Back-Hand High
Outward Strike*

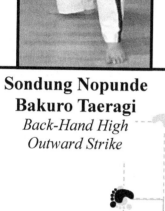

7. Move your Left foot forwards (in a stamping motion) to form a *Right L-Stance* while executing a *Back-Hand High Outward Strike* with your Left hand.

8. Execute a *High Inward Vertical Kick* to your Left palm with your Right leg.

9. Following the previous kick, *stamp* your Right foot in front to form a *Left L-Stance* while executing a *Back-Hand High Outward Strike* with your Right hand.

Previous

Moves 7, 8 & 9

Nopunde Anuro Sewo Chagi
High Inward Vertical Kick

Sang Sonbadak Soopyong Makgi
Twin Palm Horizontal Block
(Slow Motion)

Sonkal Dung Nopunde Yop Makgi
Reverse Knifehand High Side Block
(Slow Motion)

10. Execute a *High Inward Vertical Kick* to your Right palm, with your Left leg.

11. Following the previous kick, lower your Left foot in front and *slip* it forwards to form a *Right L-Stance* while executing a *Twin Palm Horizontal Block.* Perform in slow motion.

12. Move your Right foot forwards to form a *Right Walking Stance* while executing a *Reverse Knifehand High Side Block* with your Right hand. Perform in slow motion.

Previous — *Moves 10, 11 & 12*

**Sonkal Dung Kaunde
Yop Makgi**
*Reverse Knifehand
Middle Side Block*
(Slow Motion)

**Kaunde Ap
Joomok Jirugi**
Middle Forefist Punch

**Kaunde Bandae Ap
Joomok Jirugi**
*Middle Reverse
Forefist Punch*

13. Maintain your previous stance while executing a *Reverse Knifehand High Side Block* with your Left hand. Perform in slow motion.

14. Maintain your previous stance and execute a *Right Middle Forefist Punch*.

15. Maintain your previous stance and execute a *Middle Reverse Forefist Punch* with your Left fist.

Previous   *Moves 13, 14 & 15*

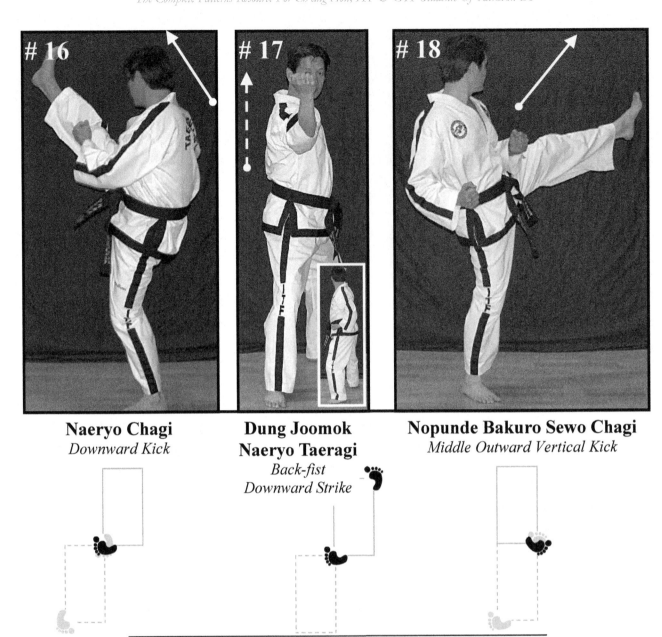

Naeryo Chagi
Downward Kick

**Dung Joomok
Naeryo Taeragi**
*Back-fist
Downward Strike*

Nopunde Bakuro Sewo Chagi
Middle Outward Vertical Kick

16. Take your weight on your Left leg and pivot 135 degrees clockwise executing a *Downward Kick* with your Right leg.

17. Following the previous kick, lower your Right foot while pivoting a further 45 degrees (clockwise - so you are now 180 degrees from move 15) and stamp to form a *Left L-Stance* while executing a *Back-fist Downward Strike* with your Right fist.

18. Take your weight on your Right leg pivot 135 degrees anti-clockwise executing a *Middle Outward Vertical Kick* with your Left leg.

Previous | Moves 16, 17 & 18

Dung Joomok **Naeryo Taeragi**	**Nopunde Bandae Ap** **Joomok Jirugi**	**Nopunde Ap** **Joomok Jirugi**
Back-fist Downward Strike	*High Reverse Forefist Punch*	*High Forefist Punch*

ITF Note: Movements 20 & 21 are performed in *'Fast Motion'*

19. Following the previous kick, lower your Left foot while pivoting a further 45 degrees (anti-clockwise) and stamp to form a *Right L-Stance* while executing a *Back-fist Downward Strike* with your Left fist.

20. Pivoting on your Left foot, turn 180 degrees clockwise, moving your Right foot to form a *Right Walking Stance* while executing a *High Reverse Punch* with your Left fist.

21. Maintain your stance and execute a *High Obverse Forefist Punch* with your Right Fist.

Previous

Moves 19, 20 & 21

**Sonmokdung
Ollyo Makgi**
Bow Wrist Upward Block

**Sonmokdung
Ollyo Makgi**
Bow Wrist Upward Block

Sonbadak Noollo Makgi
Palm Pressing Block
(Slow Motion)

  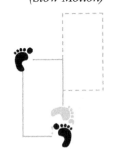

22. Move your Left foot forwards to form a *Right Rear Foot Stance* while executing a *Bow Wrist Upwards Block* with your Left wrist.

23. Move your Right foot forwards to form a *Left Rear Foot Stance* while executing a *Bow Wrist Upwards Block* with your Right wrist.

24. Taking your weight on your Right foot, pivot 180 degrees anti-clockwise. Following the turn, slide your Left foot forwards to form a *Left Walking Stance* while executing a *Left Palm Pressing Block*. Perform in slow motion.

Previous   *Moves 22, 23 & 24*

Sonbadak Noollo Makgi
Palm Pressing Block
(Slow Motion)

Circular Motion

Moa Sogi, Sonkal Najunde Ap Makgi
Closed Stance, Knifehand Low Front Block.
(Strike Left Knifehand To Right Palm)

25. Move your Right foot forwards to form a *Right Walking Stance* while executing a *Right Palm Pressing Block*. Perform in slow motion.

26a & b. Bring your rear (Left) foot to your Right foot to form a *Closed Stance* and bring both hands above your head, then downwards in a circular motion before striking your Left palm with your Right Knifehand (performing a *Knifehand Low Front Block)*.

Previous   Moves 25, 26a & 26b

Sonkal Chookyo Makgi
Knifehand Rising Block

Nopunde Bandae Ap Joomok Jirugi
High Reverse Forefist Punch

Dwijibo Jirugi
Upset Punch

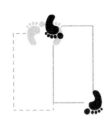

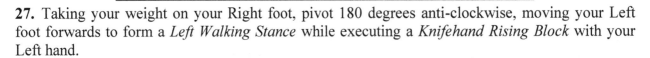

27. Taking your weight on your Right foot, pivot 180 degrees anti-clockwise, moving your Left foot forwards to form a *Left Walking Stance* while executing a *Knifehand Rising Block* with your Left hand.

28. Maintain your previous stance and execute a *High Reverse Forefist Punch* with your Right fist.

29. *Slide* forwards and move your Right foot in front to form a *Left L-Stance* while executing an *Upset Punch* with your Left fist, bringing your Right fist to the front of your Left shoulder.

Previous   *Moves 27, 28 & 29*

 # 30

 # 31

 # 32

Homi Sonkut
Nopunde Tulgi
Angle Fingertip
High Thrust

Sonkal Chookyo Makgi
Knifehand Rising Block

Nopunde Bandae Ap
Joomok Jirugi
High Reverse Forefist Punch

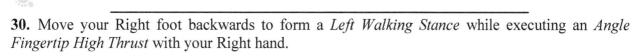

30. Move your Right foot backwards to form a *Left Walking Stance* while executing an *Angle Fingertip High Thrust* with your Right hand.

31. Perform a centre-line turn to form a *Right Walking Stance* while executing a *Knifehand Rising Block* with your Right hand.

32. Maintain your previous stance and execute a *High Reverse Forefist Punch* with your Left fist.

Previous

Moves 30, 31 & 32

Dwijibo Jirugi
Upset Punch

Homi Sonkut Nopunde Tulgi
Angle Fingertip High Thrust

Sonkal Dung Najunde Daebi Makgi
Low Reverse Knifehand Guarding Block

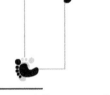

33. *Slide* forwards, moving your Left foot in front to form a *Right L-Stance* while executing an *Upset Punch* with your Right fist, bringing your Left fist to the front of your Right shoulder.

34. Move your Left foot backwards to form a *Right Walking Stance* while executing an *Angle Fingertip High Thrust* with your Left hand.

35. Without moving forwards, slip your Right foot to form a *Left L-Stance* while executing a *Low Reverse Knifehand Guarding Block*. Perform in a circular motion.

Previous　　　　　　　　　　　*Moves 33, 34 & 35*

Sonkal Dung Najunde Daebi Makgi

Low Reverse Knifehand Guarding Block

Najunde Bakat Palmok Makgi / Kaunde Sonkal Bakuro Makgi

Low Outer Forearm Block/Middle Knifehand Outward Block

Nopunde Sang Sewo Jirugi

High Twin Vertical Punch

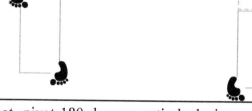

36. Taking your weight on your Right foot, pivot 180 degrees anti-clockwise, moving your Left foot to form a *Right L-Stance* while executing a *Low Reverse Knifehand Guarding Block*. Perform in a circular motion.

37. Without stepping forwards, slip your Left foot to form a *Left Walking Stance* while executing a *Right Low Outer Forearm Block* and a *Left Knifehand Outward Block* simultaneously.

38. Move your Right foot forwards (in a stamping motion) to form a *Right Walking Stance* while executing a *High Twin Vertical Fist Punch*.

Previous　　　　　　　　　　*Moves 36, 37 & 38*

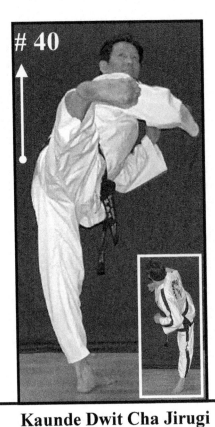

Waebal Sogi, Paldung Taeragi
One-Leg Stance, Back-Forearm Strike

Kaunde Dwit Cha Jirugi
Middle Back Piercing kick

Bakat Palmok San Makgi
Outer Forearm W Block

39. While maintaining the direction you were travelling in (per move 38), bring your Right foot back to the side of your Left knee to form a *Left One-Leg Stance*, striking your Left palm with your *Right Back-Forearm*.

40. Without lowering your Right foot, immediately execute a *Middle Back Piercing Kick* to your rear with your Right leg, pulling both your hands in the opposite direction as you execute the kick.

41. Following the kick, lower your Right foot to form a *Sitting Stance* while executing an *Outer Forearm W Block*. **Note**: Your palms face outwards on this technique.

Previous   *Moves 39, 40 & 41*

Bakat Palmok Mikulmyo San Makgi	**San Makgi**	**Bakat Palmok Mikulmyo San Makgi**
Outer Forearm Sliding W Block	*W Block*	*Outer Forearm Sliding W Block*

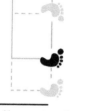

42. Slide to your Right-hand side, maintaining your previous stance while executing an *Outer Forearm W Block*. **Note**: Your palms face outwards on this technique.

43. Pivot 180 degrees anti-clockwise and stamp your Right foot into a *Sitting Stance* while executing an *Outer Forearm W Block*. **Note**: Your palms face inwards on this technique.

44. Slide to your Left-hand side, maintaining your previous stance while executing an *Outer Forearm W Block*. **Note**: Your palms face outwards on this technique.

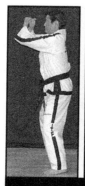

Previous   *Moves 42, 43 & 44*

**Waebal Sogi,
Paldung Taeragi**
*One-Leg Stance,
Back-Forearm Strike*

**Nopunde Dwit
Cha Jirugi**
High Back Piercing kick

**Kyocha Joomok Noollo
Makgi**
X-Fist Pressing Block

45. Pivot 90 degrees anti-clockwise on your Right foot and bring your Left foot back to the side of your Right knee to form a *Right One-Leg Stance*, striking your Right palm with your *Left Back-Forearm*.

46. Without lowering your Left foot, immediately execute a *High Back Piercing Kick* to your rear with your Left leg. Pull both your hands in the opposite direction as you execute the kick.

47. Following the previous kick and without placing the kicking foot down, jump forwards to form a *Left X-Stance* while executing a *X-Fist Pressing Block*.

Previous   *Moves 45, 46 & 47*

**Mit Joomok
Ap Taeragi**
Under Fist Front Strike

**Mit Joomok
Ap Taeragi**
*Under Fist
Front Strike*

**Kaunde Sonbadak
Miro Makgi**
Middle Palm Pushing Block

48. Move your Right foot backwards to form a *Left Walking Stance* while executing an *Under Fist Front Strike* with your Left hand.

49. Move your Right foot forwards to form a *Right Walking Stance* while executing an *Under Fist Front Strike* with your Right hand.

50. Maintain your previous stance and execute a *Middle Palm Pushing Block* with your Left hand.

Previous — *Moves 48, 49 & 50*

Sonkal Dollimyo Makgi
Knifehand Circular Block

Kaunde Sonbadak Miro Makgi
Middle Palm Pushing Block

Sonkal Dollimyo Makgi
Knifehand Circular Block

51. Pivot 135 degrees anti-clockwise on the balls of your feet to form an *angled Left Walking Stance* while executing a *Knifehand Circular Block* with your Right hand.

52. Pivot 135 degrees clockwise (to face your previous direction) whilst moving your Left foot forwards to form a *Left Walking Stance* while executing a *Middle Palm Pushing Block* with your Right palm.

53. Pivot 135 degrees clockwise on the balls of your feet to form an *angled Right Walking Stance* while executing a *Knifehand Circular Block* with your Left hand.

Previous　　　　　　　　　　　　　　　　　　*Moves 51, 52 & 53*

**Nopunde Yop
Cha Jirugi**
High Side Piercing Kick

**Sang Yop Dwi
Palkup Tulgi**
Twin Side Back Elbow Thrust

Kaunde Yop Jirugi
Middle Side Punch

54a. Execute a *High Side Piercing Kick* with your Right leg. Try to form a *Forearm Guarding Block* as you kick.

54b. Following the previous kick, lower your Right foot beside your Left foot to form a *Closed Stance* while executing a *Twin Side Back Elbow Thrust*.

55. Pivoting 90 degrees clockwise, slide your Left foot out to form a *Sitting Stance* while executing a *Middle Side Punch* with your Left fist.

Previous

Moves 51b, 52 & 53

Kaunde Bandae Ap
Joomok Jirugi
Middle Reverse Forefist Punch

Sonkal Moa
Narani Sogi*
Parallel Stance with
Overlapped Back-hand

56. Pivot on your Left foot, shifting your Right (rear) foot to form a *Left Walking Stance* while executing a *Middle Reverse Forefist Punch* with your Right fist.

Return. Move your Right foot forwards to the ready posture (*Parallel Stance with Overlapped Back-hand*).

Previous — *Move 56 & return to Ready Stance*

Tips For Tong-Il Tul

1. Ensure all slow motion techniques are performed with the same time duration.

2. Ensure the Twin Knifehand Horizontal Strike (move #2) is level.

3. When executing the Bow Wrist Blocks (moves #22 and #23), do not allow the wrist to bend to sharply.

4. The third W-Shape Block (move #43) is performed with an inward motion, but is still using outer forearm as the blocking tool.

5. Move 54 is not a Bending Ready Stance as you don't stop, although it may look similar to one - see small pictures for example.

6. For reference:

- Tong-Il means *'Unification'* which was General Choi's lifelong dream (to unite both Korea's).
- The pattern diagram of a straight line represents the *'homogenous Korean race'*, meaning (to General Choi) that there are no *'North or South Korean'* people, just *'Korean'* people.
- **Move #1** *(Twin Fist Middle Punch)* represents *'One Country'* (i.e. A single Korea)
- **Move #2** *(Twin Knifehand Horizontal Strike)* represents *'One Country Divided'* (i.e. The separating of Korea into North and South).
- **Move #3** *(Outer Forearm Middle Inward Block)* represents *'A Sudden Attack'* (i.e. Korea being invaded).
- **Move #38** *(High Twin Vertical Punch)* represents the breaking of the 38th Parallel (the line that divides North and South Korea), to make *'one country or one Korea'* again.
- The various stamping motions employed within the pattern represent General Choi's frustration and anger at Korea being a country divided.

Silla Knife Pattern

Hwa-Rang Knife Pattern

신라 단 검 틀

Introduced by Grandmaster Kim, Bok Man, the Silla (pronounced Shilla) Knife Pattern is said to have origins in the Silla Dynasty in the 7th Century. The 46 moves of this pattern emphasise speed, accuracy and proper judgement of movement, with decisive counter-attacks. This pattern is also known as the Hwa-Rang Knife pattern.

Narani Junbi Sogi
Parallel Ready Stance

Kaunde Jirugi
Middle Stab

Ready Posture. *Parallel Ready Stance* holding the knife vertical in your Right hand, with your Left hand over your Right fist.

1. From *Parallel Ready Stance,* move your Right foot out to your side to form a *Sitting Stance* while executing a *Middle Stab*, holding the knife with both hands.

From the ready posture to move 1

Kaunde Soopyong Geueigi / Kaunde Sonkal Yop Taeragi
Middle Horizontal Slash / Middle Knifehand Side Strike.

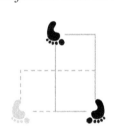

Nopunde Anuro Geueigi
High Inward Slash

2. Move your Right foot backwards to form a *Left Walking Stance* while executing a *Middle Horizontal Slash* with the knife and a *Middle Knifehand Side Strike* with your Left Knifehand.

3. Move your Right foot forwards to form a *Left L-Stance* while executing a *High Inward Slash* with the knife, bringing your *Left Side Fist* to your Right shoulder.

Previous

Moves 2 & 3

**Kaunde Soopyong
Bakuro Geueigi**
*Middle Horizontal
Outward Slash*

Kaunde Ap Cha Busigi
Middle Front Snap Kick

4. Maintain your stance but *shift* forwards and execute a *Middle Horizontal Outward Slash* with the knife.

5. Hold your arms out to the side while executing a *Middle Front Snap Kick* with your Left leg.

Previous   *Moves 4 & 5*

Kaunde Jirugi
Middle Stab

**Soopyong Geueigi
/ Kaunde Sonkal Yop Taeragi**
*Middle Horizontal Slash
/ Middle Knifehand Side Strike.*

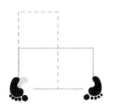

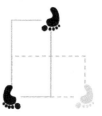

6. Following the previous kick, bring your Left foot down in-line with your Left foot to form a Sitting Stance while *passing the knife* to your Left hand and execute a *Middle Stab,* holding the knife with both hands.

7. Move your Left foot backwards to form a *Right Walking Stance* while executing a *Middle Horizontal Slash* with the knife and a *Middle Knifehand Side Strike* with your Right Knifehand.

Previous

Moves 6 & 7

Nopunde Anuro Geueigi
High Inward Slash

Kaunde Soopyong Bakuro Geueigi
Middle Horizontal Outward Slash

8. Move your Left foot forwards to form a *Right L-Stance* while executing a *High Inward Slash* with the knife, bringing your *Right Side Fist* to your Left shoulder.

9. Maintain your stance but *shift* forwards and execute a *Middle Horizontal Outward Slash* with the knife.

Previous

Moves 8 & 9

Kaunde Ap Cha Busigi
Middle Front Snap Kick

**Nopunde Sasun
Bakuro Geueigi**
*High Diagonal
Outward Slash*

10. Hold your arms out to the side while executing a *Middle Front Snap Kick* with your Right leg.

11. Following the previous kick, lower your Right foot in front to form a *Right Walking Stance* while *passing the knife* to your Right hand and execute a *High Diagonal Outward Slash* with the knife.

Previous   *Moves 10 & 11*

Kaunde Dwit Jiriugi
Middle Rear Stab

Soojik Ollyo Geueigi
Vertical Upward Slash

Kaunde Soojik Naerjo Jirugi
Middle Vertical Downward Stab

12. Move your Right foot behind you to form a *Right L-Stance* while executing a *Middle Rear Stab* with your knife, supporting the knife hilt with your Left palm.

13. Move your Right foot forwards to form a *Right Walking Stance* while executing a *Vertical Upward Slash* with the knife.

14. Move your Left foot forwards to form a *Left Walking Stance* while executing a *Middle Vertical Downward Slash* with the knife.

Previous | *Moves 12, 13 & 14*

**Kaunde Sasun
Naerjo Jirugi**
*Middle Diagonal
Downward Stab*

**Kaunde Soopyong
Anuro Geueigi**
*Middle Horizontal
Inward Slash*

Kaunde Jiriugi
Middle Stab

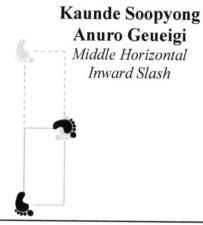

15. Maintain your stance and execute a *Middle Diagonal Downward Stab* with the knife.

16. Move your Right foot forwards to form a *Left L-Stance* while executing a *Middle Horizontal Inward Slash* with the knife.

17. Without moving, shift your Right foot to form a *Right Walking Stance* while simultaneously passing the knife to your Left hand and execute a *Middle Stab* with the knife.

Previous   *Moves 15, 16 & 17*

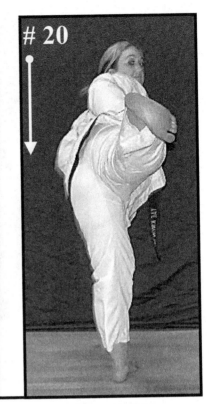

 # 18

Najunde Geueigi
Low Slash

 # 19

Nopunde Soojik Ollyo Jirugi
High Vertical Upward Stab

 # 20

Kaunde Yop Cha Jirugi
Middle Side Piercing Kick

18. Maintain your stance and execute a *Low Slash* to you Left-hand side with the knife.

19. Without moving, shift your Left foot to form a *Left L-Stance* while executing a *High Vertical Upward Stab* with the knife, simultaneously pulling your *Right Side Fist* to your Left shoulder.

20. While pulling the knife to rest on your Left hip, execute a *Middle Side Piercing Kick* with your Right leg.

Previous
Moves 18, 19 & 20

**Nopunde Soojik
Ollyo Jirugi**
*High Vertical
Upward Stab*

Kaunde Yop Cha Jirugi
Middle Side Piercing Kick

**Nopunde Sasun
Bakuro Geueigi**
*High Diagonal
Outward Slash*

21. Following the previous kick, lower your Right foot while turning 180 degrees to form a *Right L-Stance* simultaneously changing the knife to your Right hand. Execute a *High Vertical Upward Stab* with the knife, simultaneously pulling your *Left Side Fist* to your Right shoulder.

22. While pulling the knife to rest on your Right hip, execute a *Middle Side Piercing Kick* with your Left leg.

23. Following the previous kick, lower your Left foot in front to form a *Left Walking Stance*, simultaneously changing the knife to your Left hand and execute a *High Diagonal Outward Slash*.

Previous   *Moves 21, 22 & 23*

Kaunde Dwit Jiriugi
Middle Rear Stab

Soojik Ollyo Geueigi
Vertical Upward Slash

Kaunde Soojik Naerjo Jirugi
Middle Vertical Downward Stab

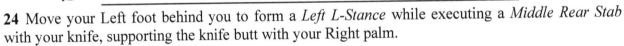

24 Move your Left foot behind you to form a *Left L-Stance* while executing a *Middle Rear Stab* with your knife, supporting the knife butt with your Right palm.

25. Move your Left foot forwards to form a *Left Walking Stance* while executing a *Vertical Upward Slash* with the knife.

26. Move your Right foot forwards to form a *Right Walking Stance* while executing a *Middle Vertical Downward Slash* with the knife.

Previous — Moves 24, 25 & 26

**Kaunde Sasun
Naerjo Jirugi**
*Middle Diagonal
Downward Stab*

**Kaunde Soopyong
Anuro Geueigi**
*Middle Horizontal
Inward Slash*

Kaunde Jirugi
Middle Stab

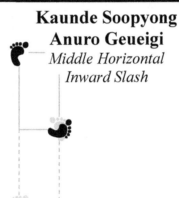

27. Maintain your stance and execute a *Middle Diagonal Downward Stab* with the knife.

28. Move your Left foot forwards to form a *Right L-Stance* while executing a *Middle Horizontal Inward Slash* with the knife.

29. Without moving, shift your Left foot to form a *Left Walking Stance* while simultaneously passing the knife to your Right hand and execute a *Middle Stab* with the knife.

Previous

Moves 27, 28 & 29

Najunde Geueigi
Low Slash

**Nopunde Sasun
Anuro Geueigi**
High Diagonal Inward Slash

**Kaunde Soopyong
Bakuro Geueigi**
*Middle Horizontal
Outward Slash*

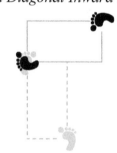

30. Maintain your stance and execute a *Low Slash* to your Right-hand side with the knife.

31. Move your Right foot half way forwards towards your Left foot then simultaneously pivot 90 degrees anti-clockwise, sliding your Right foot back out again to form a *Left Walking Stance* while executing a *High Diagonal Inward Slash* with the knife.

32. While turning 90 degrees clockwise, move your Right foot to form a *Left L-Stance* while executing a *Middle Horizontal Outward Slash* with the knife.

Previous

Moves 30, 31 & 32

**Nopunde Anuro
Naeri Chigi**

High Inward Chop

**Kaunde Naerjo
Naeri Chigi**

Middle Downward Chop

Kaunde Jirugi

Middle Stab

33. Maintain your stance and execute a *High Inward Chop* with the knife, while bringing your *Left Knifehand* in front of your Right shoulder.

34. Without moving, pull your Right foot back towards your Left foot to form a *Left Vertical Stance* while executing a *Middle Downward Chop* with the knife.

35. Slide the Right foot forwards again to form a *Left L-Stance* while executing a *Middle Stab* with the knife.

Previous   *Moves 33, 34 & 35*

Najunde Anuro Naeri Chigi
Low Inward Chop

Nopunde Sasun Anuro Geueigi
High Diagonal Inward Slash

Kaunde Soopyong Bakuro Geueigi
Middle Horizontal Outward Slash

36. Maintain your stance and execute a *Low Inward Chop* with the knife to your Left Side Front, bringing the finger belly of your Left hand to the underside (now facing upwards) of your Right forearm.

37. Move your Left foot half way forwards towards your Right foot, changing knife hands as you do so, then simultaneously pivot 90 degrees clockwise while sliding your Left foot back out again to form a *Right Walking Stance* while executing a *High Diagonal Inward Slash* with the knife.

38. Turning 90 degrees anti-clockwise, move your Left foot to form a *Right L-Stance* while executing a *Middle Horizontal Outward Slash* with the knife.

Previous   *Moves 36, 37 & 38*

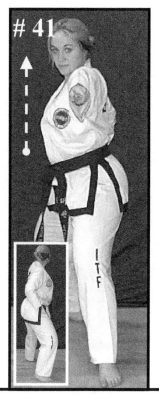

**Nopunde Anuro
Naeri Chigi**
High Inward Chop

**Kaunde Naerjo
Naeri Chigi**
Middle Downward Chop

Kaunde Jirugi
Middle Stab

39. Maintain your stance and execute a *High Inward Chop* with the knife while bringing your *Right Knifehand* in front of your Left shoulder.

40. Without moving, pull your Left foot back towards your Right foot to form a *Right Vertical Stance* while executing a *Middle Downward Chop* with the knife.

41. Slide the Left foot forwards again to form a *Right L-Stance* while executing a *Middle Stab* with the knife.

Previous   *Moves 39, 40 & 41*

**Najunde Anuro
Naeri Chigi**
Low Inward Chop

Nopunde Jirugi
High Stab

**Yangson Jirugi
Daebi Jahseh**
*Two Handed
Thrust Ready Position*

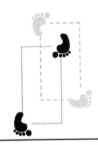

42. Maintain your stance and execute a *Low Inward Chop* with the knife to your Right Side Front, bringing the finger belly of your Right hand to the underside (now facing upwards) of your Left forearm.

43. Perform a centre-line turn to form a *Right Walking Stance* while executing a *High Stab* with the knife.

44. Without moving, shift (moving Right foot) into a *Left L-Stance* while simultaneously placing your Right hand onto your Left fist and withdraw (pull) the knife towards your belly.

Previous　　　　　　　　*Moves 42, 43 & 44*

Nopunde Jirugi
High Stab

Yangson Jirugi
Daebi Jahseh
Two Handed
Thrust Ready Position

Narani Junbi Sogi
Parallel Ready Stance

45. Pass the knife to your Right hand while moving your Left leg forwards to form a *Left Walking Stance* while executing a *High Stab* with the knife.

46. Without moving, shift (moving Left foot) into a *Right L-Stance* while simultaneously placing your Left hand onto your Right fist and withdraw (pull) the knife towards your belly.

Return. Bring your Left foot back to the Ready Posture (*Parallel Ready Stance*).

Previous — Moves 45, 46 and return to ready posture

Tips For Silla Knife Tul

1. Remember a *'Stab'* means the point of the knife hits the (imaginary) opponent. A *'Slash'* means the blade of the knife slices across the (imaginary) opponent. A *'Chop'* means the blade of the knife drives into the (imaginary) opponent.

2. Be sure to use your upper body and waist when executing the techniques, as correct twisting will generate the power to enable a slash, chop or thrust to work as intended.

3. Be aware that the knife changes hands at move #6, prior to move #11(where it is also rotated for a different grip), for move #17, following move #20, for move #23 (where it is also rotated for a different grip), for move #29, during move #37 and at move #45.

Appendices

'Glory is temporary.
Wisdom lasts forever.
Train for a deeper understanding of yourself'

Pattern Speeds
By Master Paul McPhail, 7th Degree, ITFNZ

The follow is a study of the various speeds in patterns, such as fast and continuous motion, and how the ITF perform sine wave. "In the beginning", there was only *normal*, *fast* and *slow* motion. *Continuous* came later, then finally *connecting* with the publishing of the second edition of the 15 volume Encyclopedia in 1983.

There is generally no problem with understanding slow and connecting motion... *connecting* being two movements in the one sinewave and one breath...like hooking block/punch in Yul-Gok, scooping block/punch in Ge-Baek.

But what is the difference between fast and continuous motion?
Is it the sine wave? Is it the breathing? Is it the overall speed or time it takes to complete the movements? Is it the interval of time between the two movements? Let's look at these one by one:

Sine Wave

With the *continuous motion* in Dun-Gun, General Choi gave very clear instructions to drop down after the low block, then rise up, then down on the rising block. In other words, *full sine wave*. Down-up-down. In Po-Eun however, every *continuous* movement is NOT done with full sinewave - the final "down" of the preceding movement becomes the first "down" of the next. So there is no clear rule there. There is also the fast motion in Ul-Ji which is just one movement - dropping into x-stance...so how can we make a clear rule to do with sinewave? Then there is fast motion with kicks also - like in Hwa-Rang and Choong-Moo...

The ITF Technical Committee also offered this definition of *continuous motion* and *sine wave* at the seminar in New Zealand, August 2004: Movements in *continuous motion* should be completed using *full sine wave* (down-up-down) unless there are more than 2 movements (eg Po-Eun 6-12, 24-30 and Yoo-Sin 16-19), in which case perform a *2/3 sine wave*. This definition holds true on my chart in the Sine wave study displayed later.

Breathing

Both *fast* and *continuous* movements call for individual breaths...although the General tended to "merge" his breaths somewhat on continuous motion. The ITF

Technical Committee further explained *continuous motion* breathing as inhaling only once, then breathing out on each technique as you execute it. (NZ seminar, August 2004). *Connecting motion* has only one breath.

It should be noted (just to confuse things) that there appears to be a mistake in the Encyclopedia. It says in the *Theory of Power* section that each movement should have one breath except for *"continuous motion"*. This I think is an error, as it states in the Training Secret section *"except on connecting motion"*.

Over-all Speed or Time Taken

Sometimes *continuous* movements take longer to complete than *fast* - sometimes the other way around. For example, the two *fast motion* punches in Do-San are over and done with quicker than the low/rising blocks in Dan-Gun. Yet in Po-Eun, the *continuous motion* techniques are completed at a fast rate.

Interval Between Movements

There is a popular view that the difference between *normal*, *fast* and *continuous* is the interval, or gap BETWEEN the movements. The idea is that two movements performed at *normal speed* would have a natural count or gap between them, *fast* has this gap shortened, the *continuous* has no gap at all. This would fine except that this is not the way *fast motion* gets performed, either by seniors, Masters or General Choi himself. If you watch, there is no gap at all between the two punches in Do-san for example... as soon as the first is finished you spring straight up into the 2nd... almost in a *continuous-like* motion.

In my discussions with General Choi, I came across what I think it is all about. I asked him - *"why not just get rid of Continuous and just call everything Fast? Don't you mean just go fast - join them together - cut out the interval between movements?"*

"No no - fast motion is performed with urgency, - aggressive. Continuous motion is performed with grace and beauty - it must flow." he replied.

So I think then, we have to try and understand what his thoughts were when he introduced the terminology. He had *"fast motion"* already - but it didn't adequately describe the flowing, continuous nature by which he wanted certain other movements linked. I don't believe he gave that much thought to there being any confusion over the two terms, as in his mind they are totally different.

If you look then...continuous movements always involve defence - and the idea is to link them smoothly with a nice flow and rhythm. Fast techniques are normally attacks, nearly always punches and kicks (but not always - Yoo Sin 34-35).

Okay, that's all very well, until you have to teach your 1st dans Ge-Baek, where we have *fast* then *continuous* motion side by side. I tend to give a few guidelines, which make people feel more comfortable with the differences. This then is the general summary I use:

Conclusion

Slow Motion - movement is performed slowly with slow breathing. This is used to emphasize an important movement and to check balance and control.

Fast Motion - urgent and aggressive, normal breathing. Fast motion is nearly always attacks - mainly two punches. Short-cut your sine wave - spring straight from the first movement into the next.

Continuous Motion - link the movements together with no pause between the end of one movement and the start of the next. Breath in once then out in a continuous flow of air but emphasizing each movement. Try to link the moments smoothly, with grace and beauty. (Continuous movements always start with a block).

Connecting Motion - complete the two movements with one breath and one sine wave. Connecting motion is always with two movements using opposite arms.

There is also other terminology used in patterns like - ***"in a quick motion, a releasing motion, in a consecutive kick"*** etc. How is a *quick motion* different from a *fast motion*? I asked the General is it the same... he laughed and said *"no no"* ...but gave no explanation!

My thoughts with these are:

- ***"Releasing Motion"***, the General is telling us it is a releasing technique.

- ***"Consecutive Kick"***, the General is telling us *"do not put your foot on the ground after the first kick".*

- ***"Quick"*** - used for single movements so means *"do it quickly",* as opposed *to fast motion*, which describes how two or more movements should be performed together.

Pattern Orders of Taekwon-Do Organisations

All organisations that have a link back to General Choi and the Ch'ang Hon patterns utilize them as part of their training and gradings. However, certain organisations have them in different orders due to the time they either left the ITF or for other reasons for example the way their Chief Instructor may have learned them. These lists represent the pattern orders of various big Taekwon-do organisations, with further breakaway groups usually following the exact same sequence.

The following organisational lists appear on the next few pages:

International Taekwon-Do Federation (ITF)
For ITF and Ch'ang Hon organisations that follow the ITF order of patterns.

Global Taekwon-Do Federation (GTF)
For GTF and other organisations that follow the patterns as directed by the late Grandmaster Park, Jung Tae.

Action International Martial Arts Association (AIMAA)
For AIMAA students and other organisations those that follow the patterns as directed by the Grandmaster Hee, Il Cho.

Grandmaster Jhoon Rhee
For students of Grandmaster Jhoon Rhee and organisations that follow the same order of patterns.

Grade	ITF	GTF
10th Kup	Saju Jirugi, Saju Makgi	Saju Jirugi, Saju Makgi
9th Kup	Chon-Ji	Chon-Ji
8th Kup	Dan-Gun	Dan-Gun, Jee-Sang
7th Kup	Do-San	Do-San
6th Kup	Won-Hyo	Won-Hyo, Dhan-Goon
5th Kup	Yul-Gok	Yul-Gok
4th Kup	Joong-Gun	Joong-Gun
3rd Kup	Toi-Gye	Toi-Gye
2nd Kup	Hwa-Rang, Saju-Tulgi	Hwa-Rang
1st Kup	Choong-Moo	Choong-Moo
1st Degree	Kwang-Gae, Po-Eun, Ge-Baek	Kwang-Gae, Po-Eun, Ge-Baek, Jee-Goo
2nd Degree	Eui-Am, Choong-Jang, Ko-Dang <u>or</u> Ju-Che	Eui-Am, Choong-Jang Ko-Dang, Jook-Am
3rd Degree	Sam-Il, Yoo-Sin, Choi-Yong	Sam-Il, Yoo-Sin, Choi-Yong, Pyong-Hwa
4th Degree	Yong-Gae, Ul-Ji, Moon-Moo	Yong-Gae, Ul-Ji, Moon-Moo, Sun-Duk
5th Degree	So-San, Se-Jong	So-San, Se-Jong
6th Degree	Tong-Il	Tong-Il
7th Degree		
8th Degree		

Grade	AIMAA	GM Jhoon Rhee
10th Kup	Chon-Ji	
9th Kup	Dan-Gun	
8th Kup	Do-San	Chon-Ji
7th Kup	Won-Hyo	Dan-Gun
6th Kup	Yul-Gok	Do-San
5th Kup	Joong-Gun	Won-Hyo
4th Kup	Toi-Gye	Yul-Gok
3rd Kup	Hwa-Rang	Joong-Gun
2nd Kup	Choong-Moo	Toi-Gye, Hwa-Rang
1st Kup	Kwang-Gae	Choong-Moo, Chul-Gi*
1st Degree	Po-Eun	Kwang-Gae, Basai*
2nd Degree	Ge-Baek	Po-Eun, Sip-Soo*, Bo-Ichi* or Tonfa-Ichi*
3rd Degree	Yoo-Sin	Ge-Baek, Won-Kan*
4th Degree	Choong-Jang, Ul-Ji	Choi-Yong
5th Degree	Ko-Dang, Sam-Il	* Chul-Gi is Tekki Kata, Basai is Basai-Dai Kata, Sip-Soo is Jitte Kata - all found in Shotokan Karate, Won-Kan is an Okinawan Shorin-Ryu kata and Bo-Ichi/Tonfa-Ichi are Okinawan Kobudo kata's.
6th Degree	Choi-Yong	
7th Degree	Se-Jong	** The above list is based on the forms that Grandmaster Jhoon Rhee taught from 1968 onwards, he has since introduced new forms that he terms *'Martial Arts Ballet'* - these are Kyu-Yool, Kumsa, Jayoo, Chosang, Jung-Yee, Pyung-Fa, 'Might for Right' and 'Marriage of East to West' - *unfortunately, all the above are beyond the scope of these books*
8th Degree	Tong-Il	

Kihaps In Patterns

Some, but not all Ch'ang Hon based Taekwon-Do organisations require students to Kihap (Spirit shout) at certain points within the patterns they are performing. The following charts list the various points within the patterns where Kihaps are executed, as detailed by very high ranking and respected Masters within Taekwon-Do and serve as a reference guide for those that practice patterns with Kihaps.

Cross-Referencing

The following charts have been compiled from research and cross-referencing the Kihap points used (or not) by the following Masters of Taekwon-Do:

General Choi, Hong Hi - As the founder of Ch'ang Hon Taekwon-Do and its patterns, research seems to indicate that *'unofficially'* Kihaps were allowed to be performed within the patterns. Despite this the General did not list any Kihap points at all in his books published between 1959 and 1999. Therefore Kihaps were never *'officially'* part of Ch'ang Hon Taekwon-Do or the ITF. It should be noted that, as far as I`m aware, it was always customary to Kihap on completion of a pattern (the last movement), possibly a *'knock on'* effect from Karate. This continued until some time in the early 1980's, when General Choi made it mandatory for those in the ITF to shout the name of the pattern instead of a Kihap, as well as formerly stating that there were to be no more Kihaps executed within the patterns.

Grandmaster Kang, Suh Chong - Originally a student under the Chung Do Kwan under its founder, Grandmaster Lee, Won Kuk and an instructor in the ROK army from 1960 to 1968. Vice president of the ITF from 1977 to 1983. As far as I am aware Grandmaster Kang is still teaching Taekwon-Do in the USA. Grandmaster Kang's Kihap points are referenced from Chon-Ji up to Tong-Il and include both Ko-Dang and Juche.

Grandmaster Kim, Bok Man - A military instructor with the ROK army from 1950 to 1962, Grandmaster Kim obtained the highest non-commissioned officer rank of Sgt. Major. He assisted General Choi in formulating at least 15 of the Ch'ang Hon patterns and further went on to formulate more patterns of his own. These patterns included weapons patterns and he developed his own system of martial art known as *'Chun Kuhn Do'*. Grandmaster Kim's Kihap points are referenced from Chon-Ji, up the 2nd degree patterns and include Ko-dang but not Juche.

Grandmaster Park, Jung Tae - Former ITF Secretary-General and Chairman of the ITF Instruction Committee from 1984 until he left to form the GTF in 1990.

Grandmaster Park played a major role in formulating the pattern *'Juche'* as well as being the main instructor chosen to teach Taekwon-Do in North Korea. He continued to develop his own patterns for the GTF until he passed away in 2002. Grandmaster Park did not teach any Kihap points for the Ch'ang Hon patterns. He has one Kihap point only and it appears in the GTF pattern *'Jook-Am'* (on the 360 degree Reverse Turning Kick). GTF students also shout the name on completion of a pattern, rather than Kihap. Grandmaster Park is an important inclusion in this research due to his former positions within the ITF as well as the fact that he knew and has taught all 25 Ch'ang Hon patterns and didn't teach any Kihaps in them at all.

Grandmaster Rhee, Jhoon Goo - Commonly recognised as the *'Father of American Taekwon-Do'*, he trained at the Chung Do Kwan under Grandmaster Nam, Tae Hi and moved to the USA in 1952. Grandmaster Rhee's Kihap points are referenced from Chon-Ji to Choong-Moo and it is unknown whether he included them in higher grade patterns.

Grandmaster Lim, Won Sup and Grandmaster Lee, Myung Woo - Two pioneering Taekwon-Do instructors who taught in Vietnam. Their combined list was supplied by my good friend Yi, Yun Wook who learned from them while training in Vietnam. Grandmaster Lim (who was part of the ITF until about 1984) replaced Grandmaster Park as the instructor for North Korea) and Grandmaster Lee's combined list references Kihap points from Chon-Ji up to the 1st degree patterns.

Grandmaster Hee, Il Cho - Grandmaster Cho is a well known and respected Taekwon-Do Grandmaster and pioneer. He has authored numerous books and videos on Taekwon-Do, as well as featuring in movies. Grandmaster Cho taught Taekwon-Do to Special Forces soldiers (Korea, India and US) during the 1960's before emigrating to the US in 1968. In the 1980's he was the black belt grading examiner for the TAGB, then in the 1990's he became the Black Belt grading examiner for the GTI. He runs his own organisation (AIMAA) which is respected worldwide. Grandmaster Cho's Kihap points are referenced for the 20 original patterns and do not include Eui-Am, Juche, Moon-Moo, Yon-Gae and So-San.

Grandmaster Choi, Jung Hwa - Grandmaster Choi is the son of the founder of Taekwon-Do (General Choi) and current President of ITF-Canada. He is thought to have helped Grandmaster Park formulate pattern Juche. Though not one of the original Pioneers, Grandmaster Choi is an important figure in Taekwon-Do, however his inclusion in this appendix is even more important as in 2008 he decided to re-introduce Kihaps back into the patterns performed by ITF-C members. Grandmaster Choi's Kihap points are referenced from Chon-Ji up to the 1st degree patterns only because, at the time of writing, the ITF-C has only issued points up to 1st degree, though more have been expected for a while now.

Note: Other ITF groups do not perform these Kihaps, but simply shout the name of the pattern on completion.

Pattern	GM Lim, Won Sup	GM Kim, Bok Man	GM Choi, Jung Hwa (ITF-C)	GM Hee, Il Cho (AIMAA)	GM Jhoon Rhee	GM Kang, Suh Chong
Chon-Ji	#17	#19	#17	#19	#1, #8, #19	#1, #17, #19
Dan-Gun	#8, #17	#8, #21	#8, #17	#8, #17	#1, #8, #21	#1 #8, #17, #19
Do-San	#6	#6, #24	#6, #22	#6, #24	#1, #6, #24	#2, #6, #22, #24
Won-Hyo	#12, #26	#12, #27	#12	#12, #26	#1, #12, #28	#1, #12, #26
Yul-Gok	#27, #36	#21, #36	#24, #27, #36	#24, #36	#21, #36, #38	#0*, #21, #36 #38
Joong-Gun	#12	#12	#12	None	#1, #12, #32	#1, #12, #32
Toi-Gye	#21	#21, #37	#29	#21, #37	#1, #21, #37	#1, #21, #29, #37
Hwa-Rang	#25	#14, #27	#14, #25	#14 & #25	#1, #14, #29	#0*, #12a, #25, #29
Choong-Moo	#9b	#9b, #30	#9b, #19	#9b, #30	#1, #9b, #19, #30	#9a, #12, #19, #32
Kwang-Gae	#31	#23, #27, #35, #39	#23, #27	None	NA	#0*, #12, #31, #39
Po-Eun	#12 & #30	#12 & #30	#12 & #30	None	NA	#1, #18, #36
Ge-Baek	#23, #28	#26, #44	#19, #28	#23, #28	NA	#1, #28, #44

#0* denotes a Kihap placement prior or during the first movement. For Yul-Gok and Hwa-Rang a Kihap is executed prior to the first move of the pattern, for Kwang-Gae a Kihap is performed at the first part of the first movement, when breaking from Heaven Hand with two Knifehand Strikes.

 # a or b denotes a Kihap placement during a move that has one count, but is actually two or more movements, such as the Flying Side Piercing Kick and landing with a Knifehand Guarding Block in Choong-Moo. Please reference the relevant pattern chapters for clarification.

Pattern	GM Lim, Won Sup	GM Kim, Bok Man	GM Choi, Jung Hwa (ITF-C)	GM Hee, Il Cho (AIMAA)	GM Jhoon Rhee	GM Kang, Suh Chong
Ko-Dang	None	#29	NA	None	NA	#27, #37, #39
Eui-Am	None	#45	None	NA	NA	#1, #45
Choong-Jang	None	#8, #50 & #52	None	None	NA	#1, #8, #12, #19, #41, #52
Juche	NA	NA	None	NA	NA	#12b, #24b, #37d, #45
Sam-Il	None	None	None	None	NA	#1, #12, #17b, #33
Yoo-Sin	None	None	None	None	NA	#1, #38, #68
Choi-Yong	None	None	None	None	NA	#1, #46
Yong-Gae	None	None	None	NA	NA	#1, #49
Ul-Ji	None	None	None	None	NA	#1, #6, #12, #17, #27, #33, #42
Moon-Moo	None	None	None	NA	NA	#58,
So-San	None	None	None	NA	NA	#1, #28, #51b, #56b, #72
Se-Jong	None	None	None	None	NA	#1, #7, #21, #24
Tong-Il	None	None	None	None	NA	#17, #19, #38, #56

Research

Further research into the Kihaps points in the Ch'ang Hon tul seems to indicate that rather than being formerly instituted by General Choi himself, the Kihaps used by most instructors are most likely to have been carried forward from previous Karate training and placed within the Ch'ang Hon tul by personal preference and sharing by various Masters. This seems to explain why some Kihaps are in the same place while others are not. I have come to this conclusion due to the discrepancies in their location from Master to Master (which you will see on the lists), as well as information from pioneering masters such as Master CK Choi. If they were *'officially'* instituted by General Choi himself, everyone would be performing them at the same point within each pattern.

Due to the lack of standardization in Taekwon-Do, which didn't occur until the late 1970's/early 80's, this simply carried on until Kihaps were officially removed from the patterns by General Choi once standardisation of the Ch'ang Hon patterns began. However many Masters kept them either because they had left General Choi by then or simply because of personal preference.

To further complicate matters, in interviews with Master George Vitale, Grandmaster CK Choi (who helped design Ge-Baek tul) said that when it was formulated it did not include Kihaps. Grandmaster Park, Jong Soo also has said that General Choi didn't teach Kihaps when instructing patterns. Grandmaster Park lived with General Choi (in his house) in 1965 when General Choi was finalizing his English version of his book and he worked on all the patterns and photographs within the book. Though some instructors did them due to their former karate training, Grandmaster Cho, Sang Min, a 5th dan in 1968 and instructor at the official ITF Instructors course at that time confirmed that Kihaps were used when a pattern finished. This coincides with changing the Kihap at the end to shouting the name of the pattern instead.

If you don't perform Kihaps and wish to know more about them, as well as 'Ki' itself and how it relates to Taekwon-Do there is a fantastic appendix in my first book *(Ch'ang Hon Taekwon-do Hae Sul)* written by my good friend Yi, Yun Wook that goes into a lot of detail about it.

Appendix iv
Sine Wave Study
By Master Paul McPhail, 7th Degree, ITFNZ

This is an analysis of how sine wave is performed in pattern movements in relation to *fast*, *continuous* and *connecting* motion. This is based on watching General Choi and others perform the movement at various seminars over the years. There seems to be 4 ways of moving from one movement on to the next, as listed below:

Full Sine Wave - This means once the first movement is complete, you then drop your weight down, up, then down again as you complete the next movement (down/up/down).

2/3 Sine Wave - This means completing the first movement, moving straight up then down to complete the next movement (up/down).

1/3 Sine Wave - This means you are already up at the completion of the first movement, so then drop down into the next (down).

Continuous Motion	Moves	Full	2/3	1/3	None
Dan-Gun	13-14 (low block/rising block)	X			
Toi-Gye	7-8 (pressing blk/vertical punch)	X			
Po-Eun	6-12, 24-30 (blocks-punches)		X		
Ge-Baek	5-6 (rising block, low block)	X			
Ge-Baek	37-38 (low guarding blocks)	X			
Eui-Am	5-6, 18-19 (down blk/rising blk)	X			
Sam-Il	30-31 (inward block/punch)	X			
Yoo-Sin	16-17, 18-19 (hook block/punch)		X		
Yoo-Sin	20-21, 25-26 (pressing blk/rising				
Ul-Ji	2-3 (pressing block/rising block)	X			
So-San	52-53, 57-58 (low block/punch)	X			
So-San	71-72 (knifehand guarding blk/	X			

Fast Motion	Moves	Full	2/3	1/3	None
Do-San	15-16, 19-20 (punches)		X		
Yul-Gok	2-3, 5-6 (punches)		X		
Yul-Gok	9-10,13-14 (punches)		X		
Joong-Gun	15-16,18-19 (release/punch)		X		
Hwa-Rang	18-19 (turn-kick/turn-kick/KHGB)	X (block)			X (kicks)
Choong-Moo	14-15 (turn-kick/back-kick)				X
Ge-Baek	3-4 (punches)		X		
Ge-Baek	22-23 (turn-kick/flying side kick)				X
Choong-Jang	46-47 (punches)		X		
Yoo-Sin	2-3 (angle punches)		X		
Yoo-Sin	34-35, 36-37 (dbl forearm/low blk)				X
Choi Yong	21-22 (pressing blocks)		X		
Ul-Ji	11 (X-stance drop)			X	
So-San	5-6, 7-8 (Knifehand Block/punch)		X		
So-San	39-40, 47-48 (punches)		X		
Tong-Il	5-6 (punches)		X		
Tong-Il	14-15 (punches)		X		
Tong-Il	20-21 (punches)		X		

Connecting	Moves	Full	2/3	1/3	None
Yul-Gok	16-17, 19-20 (hooking/punch)			X	
Ge Baek	9-10, 29-30 (scoop/punch)			X	
Yoo-Sin	10-11, 14-15 (scoop block/punch)			X	
Moon-Moo	28-29, 37-38 (scoop block/punch)			X	

It is apparent from studying this chart that there is no direct correlation between the speed of the movement (i.e. fast, continuous or connecting motion) and how the sine wave in the movement is performed.

Thanks to Mr Mark Banicevich, IV Dan, for his assistance with this study.

Appendix v
Performers Biographies

Gordon Slater, 6th Degree

Gordon started Taekwon-Do in February, 1983 with the UKTA (United Kingdom Taekwon-Do Association), gaining his 1st degree in August 1987 with the TAGB (Tae Kwon Do Association of Great Britain) after waiting a year longer to grade due to transferring associations.

Gaining his 6th degree with the GTI (Global Taekwon-Do International) in October, 2009 he has, on his journey been the 1995 GTI English patterns and destruction champion, as well as consistently winning gold medals in patterns and destruction throughout the 90's.

During his time in Taekwon-Do he has been part of various Taekwon-Do organisations such as the UKTA (United Kingdom Taekwon-Do Association), TAGB Tae Kwon Do Association of Great Britain), ITS (Independent Taekwondo Schools) but is happy with his current association the GTI (Global Taekwon-Do International) where he is Grading Examiner, qualified referee and umpire. He has also trained in Wing-Chun Kung Fu, Karate, Kick Boxing and Boxing.

I first met Gordon around 2003 at a tournament in Kent, UK, one that we went to many times over the years, both as instructors and competitors. Indeed we have both fielded students against each other in the various divisions, as well as competed against each other in patterns, sparring and destruction divisions over the years. I asked him to be part of these books because of my high regards for him, both as a person and due to his skills in Taekwon-Do.

Gordon demonstrates the patterns Yong-Gae, So-San, Se-Jong and Tong-Il. More information on Gordon can be found at *www.essextkd.co.uk*

Stuart Anslow, 5th Degree

Stuart started Taekwon-Do early in 1991 under David Bryan (now 6th degree) and

John Pepper (who has now retired from Taekwon-Do). He graded his kup grades with the BUTF (British United Taekwon-Do Federation), gaining his 1st degree in 1994. He continued with the BUTF (which rejoined the ITF for a period) through to 2nd degree before parting ways and going solo. During this solo period he established his school; *Rayners Lane Taekwon-do Academy* in 1999, as well as taking his 3rd degree in 2000, 4th degree in 2005, before finally achieving his current grade of 5th degree in 2010 under legendary Taekwon-Do pioneer, Master Willie Lim, 8th degree.

Having had a good career in competition, culminating in World gold and silver medals in 2000, his main focus has been running his school and promoting Taekwon-Do. Further information can be found in the 'About The Author' section of this book or at the academy web site *www.raynerslanetkd.com*

Stuart demonstrates the patterns Yul-Gok, Juche, Sam-Il, Yoo-Sin, Choi-Yong, Pyong-Hwa, Ul-Gi, Moon-Moo and Sun-Duk.

Elliott Walker, 3rd Degree

Elliott started Taekwon-Do in 1989, aged 15, where he trained with Mr Brian Williams (6th degree) the senior instructor for the TAGB clubs in the North West of England. When just a 7th kup he joined the British Army, but continued training whenever he could at various clubs around the UK gaining excellent experience of the various associations and clubs. He continued to grade through the kup ranks within the TAGB up to 2nd kup, being graded by such TAGB notables as Master Don Atkins, Master Ron Sergiew, Master Kenny Walton and Dorian Bytom, before taking his 1st kup with his original instructor Brian Williams, with the (then) newly formed North West TaeKwonDo.

Achieving his 1st degree in 1996, he then started instructing and continued to grade up to his present rank of 3rd degree, which he achieved in 2005.

Having been posted to Germany in 1993 whilst with the British Army, he trained with a WTF club for a year which enabled him to practice and learn the way the WTF like to kick, again improving his overall knowledge of Taekwon-Do. In 1998 he visited Canada whilst with the army, training at local ITF style clubs to increase his skills further.

When the British Army formed the AMAA (Army Martial Arts Association), he was selected for the British Army team and remained a team member until he left the forces, being awarded Army Colours every year for this achievement. Whilst in the British Army team he was both patterns and sparring champion several times and helped the Army Team to become Inter-Service Champions over several different years. Elliott left the army in 2002 to further his Taekwon-Do instruction and now teaches 5 times a week at his schools in Kent, UK.

I first met Elliott at the 'Kick It' tournaments in 2000. I recall at the time, someone told me my next competitor in the black belt sparring was on the Army Taekwon-Do squad, so I was thinking it was going to be a heavy contact, rough and tough type of bout. Much to my surprise, Elliott was more a classy fighter and didn't go the snot and blood route as he didn't need to and it made the bout a great game of 'cat and mouse'. Over the years we have competed on numerous occasions and our friendship truly underlines one of my sayings (regarding competitions) of: *'2 minutes of war, friends for life'.* A tough fighter and a great technician - these are the reasons I asked Elliott to be part of these books.

Elliott demonstrates pattern Ko-Dang. More information on Elliott can be found at *www.kent-taekwondo.co.uk*

Vikram Gautam, 3rd Degree

Vikram started Taekwon-Do when he was just aged 10 years old (in 1991). As a child he trained with my instructors Mr. David Bryan, 6th Degree and Mr. John Pepper, 2nd Degree at Wembley Taekwon-Do School, which was part of the BUTF (British United Taekwon-do Federation). He continued to train at this Wembley Taekwon-Do School under the exceptional guidance of Mr. David Bryan and Mr. John Pepper for the next 9 years achieving his 1st degree in 2000. Following his 1st degree he began assisting me at Rayners Lane Taekwon-Do Academy and eventually started training there full time due to university making it impossible to train at his former club due to conflicts in times. Vikram graded to 2nd degree in March 2006 and for 3rd degree in 2010 under legendary Taekwon-Do pioneer, Master Willie Lim, 8th degree.

I remember Vikram as a child student who was always inquisitive and eager to learn new stuff, so much so it seems he used to ask me to teach him a new kick every class. When he first competed as a blue belt, he stole the golds in both patterns and sparring and has continued in a similar vein ever since. Following his 1st degree, he competed and fought a Karate black belt who had turned his hand to Taekwon-Do and the fight ended within about 3 seconds as Vikram landed a superb flying back piercing kick as his first technique, which although controlled, hit his opponent straight in the face ending it as a TKO! Vikram's superb natural ability and technique is why I asked him to be part of these books.

Vikram demonstrates the patterns Do-San, Toi-Gye, Choong-Moo, Jee-Goo and Eui-Am.

Colin Avis, 2nd Degree

Colin began practicing Taekwon-Do in 2001 at Rayners Lane Academy and has trained there ever since. After around five years of training he attained the grade of 1st Degree in 2006. Having reached the coveted black belt ranks, Colin maintained the same work ethic he displayed during his formative coloured belt years up to 1st degree, swiftly achieving the rank of 2nd Degree in 2008. Colin was the first student of Rayners Lane Taekwon-Do Academy to be promoted all the way from 10th Kup to 2nd Degree.

Although a student of the Academy, Colin also assists in teaching and has done so for a number of years. He can always be seen supporting the Academy's endeavours in hosting and attending numerous seminars, tournaments etc. Colin is also a seasoned competitor himself and has won his fair share of silverware, with one of the highlights being a silver medal won for sparring at the world championships hosted by Grandmaster Hee Il Cho. He was also part of the Rayners Lane Men Sparring Team that took the silver at the same World Championships.

Colin has won more 'Student of the Month' awards than any other student, as well a being the only Academy student to ever have been named 'Student of the Year' on more than one occasion, winning it in both 2004 and 2007. Colin's passion for the art, commitment and consistency to both training and the Academy as well as his technical skills are why I asked him to be part of these books.

Colin demonstrates Saju Jirugi and Saju Tulgi, as well as patterns Won-Hyo, Hwa-rang, Ge-Baek, Choong-Jang and Jook-Am.

Lyndsey Reynolds, 2nd Degree

Lyndsey started training in Taekwon-do at Rayners Lane Academy in 2000, gaining her 1st Degree in March 2008 and in doing so, became the first female student to attain a dan grade at the Academy. She became the Academy's 'Student of the Year' in 2002 and still trains as diligently as she always has. Lyndsey graded for 2nd degree in 2011.

As a white belt, her first ever competition was a World Championships in 2000 and since then she has had a good competition career and is a fearsome fighter. Her most notable tournament success was at the 2004 World Championships where she achieved a gold in sparring, a silver in patterns and a further gold as part of the Rayners Lane female team in the team sparring division.

At Rayners Lane all students are equal and thus the girls mix it up with the boys which has transcended further for Lyndsey over the years with a memorable moment being when she was a yellow belt and there were no other ladies entered in her sparring division. The event organiser gave her the choice of a straight gold or fighting in the mens division. She chose the latter and despite some tough opponents took the bronze! This happened again recently as a black belt as well! Lyndsey's skills, guts and steadfast determination is why I asked her to be part of these books.

Lyndsey demonstrates the Silla Knife Form.

Parvez Sultan, 1st Degree

Parvez started Taekwon-Do in January 2000 at Rayners Lane Academy. Always training hard, he achieved his 1st degree in 2006 along side 'Slumdog Millionaire' start Dev Patel amongst others, making them the first students of the Academy to go from white to black belt. He also won the Academy's 'Student of the Year' award in 2001.

Parvez has had a good competition career winning many medals along the way, with his highlights being the World Championships in 2004 where, after a terrible first day at the event, he pulled it together for day 2 and won the combined middle and heavyweight brown/red belt sparring division, fighting some tremendous fighters along the way. One of his proudest moments was testing himself at the authors previous organisations tournament (the BUTF British Championships) and winning the gold in the mens senior kup division after many good fights, actually ending up facing a club mate in the finals who had come up on the other side of the table.

Through the years Parvez has been a dedicated student throughout the years, training hard and showing good skills and technique, which is why I asked him to be part of these books.

Parvez demonstrates the patterns Jee-Sang and Po-Eun.

Sushil Punj, 1st Degree

Sushil started Taekwon-Do at the Academy in 1999 at just 8 years old. After achieving his 2nd Kup he took a hiatus from training, returning to take his 1st Kup, before taking his 1st degree in April, 2009 at just 17 years old. He has competed in both national and international tournaments including a World Championships in 2004.

As a child student, Sushil unfortunately failed his 2nd kup grading and stopped training, as many young students do after such disappointments, however, unlike others he showed true indomitable spirit by resuming training a few years later being older and wiser, with a brand new and intense focus taking him passed the grading he previously failed and to 1st degree, making him one of the few black belts to have come from the Academy which are the reasons I asked Sushil to be part of these books.

Sushil demonstrates the patterns Chon-Ji, Dhan-Goon, Joong-Gun and Kwang-Gae.

Kate Barry, 1st Kup

Kate started training at Rayners Lane Taekwon-do Academy just after it was founded in April 1999 and has trained there ever since. At the time of writing these books, Kate was a 2nd kup. Now a 1st kup and due to take her black belt grading 2011, despite a nagging knee problem that has slowed her progress down.

Kate has competed in many tournaments over the years including two World Championships where she won a silver in points sparring, a bronze in continuous sparring and a gold as part of the women's team in the open grade team sparring divisions, but her most memorable moment comes from a competition when she was an 8th kup where, following a previous training session that involved practising front leg side kicks to score quickly, she employed what she had practised in extra time and as soon as the ref said 'sijak' she hit her opponent with the technique, not only scoring the winning point but also lifting them off the floor and back with the kick.

Kate is the longest 'still in training' student from the Academy, having been there from the early days. Always supportive of the Academy, a hard worker and a long term student are the reasons I asked Kate to be part of these books.

Kate features in the *'Differences Between Organisations'* section of the book, as well as being one of the main photographers.

Marek Handzel, 1st Kup

Marek started Taekwon-Do in September 2004 before joining Rayners Lane Taekwon-Do Academy in February 2005. At the time of writing these books he was a 2nd Kup. He is now a 1st kup and due to take his black belt grading in 2011.

His favourite achievement to date is achieving the *'Student of the year'* award in 2006. Marek has been an exceptional student throughout the years and truly epitomises the tenet of 'perseverance', which is why I asked him to be part of these books.

Marek demonstrates pattern Dan-Gun.

Jonathan Choi, 1st Kup

Jonathan started training at Rayners Lane Taekwon-Do Academy in 2007 and at the time of writing these books he was a 2nd Kup. He is now a 1st kup and due to take his black belt grading in 2011.

A highlight of his training so far was taking home two golds at his first ever tournament. As well as Taekwon-Do Jonathan has a passion for Wushu and was also part of the WTF for a short period whilst in China. Jonathan has also won the Academy's *'Student of the Year'* award in 2008. Jonathan trains hard and is a consummate student which is why I asked him to be part of these books.

Jonathan demonstrates Saju Makgi.

Richard Baker, 1st Kup

Richard started training at Rayners Lane Taekwon-Do Academy in December, 2006 and at the time of writing these books he was a 2nd Kup. He is now a 1st kup and due to take his black belt grading in 2011.

Richard has a good competition record so far, bringing home golds in both patterns and sparring divisions. Richard always gives 110% in training and is a good student which is why I asked him to be part of these books. Richard is due to take his black belt in 2011.

Richard features in the *'Differences Between Organisations'* section of the book.

CPSIA information can be obtained
at www.ICGtesting.com
Printed in the USA
BVOW07s1701020816

R7246700001B/R72467PG457050BVX7B/2/P

9 781906 628185